THE
WISDOM
WHEEL

ALSO BY ALBERTO VILLOLDO

*The Heart of the Shaman**

*Courageous Dreaming**

Dance of the Four Winds (with Erik Jendresen)

The First Story Ever Told (with Erik Jendresen)

*The Four Insights**

Healing States (with Stanley Krippner, Ph.D.)

*The Illumination Process**

Island of the Sun (with Erik Jendresen)

Millennium: Glimpses into the 21st Century

*One Spirit Medicine**

*Power Up Your Brain** (with David Perlmutter, M.D.)

The Realms of Healing (with Stanley Krippner, Ph.D.)

Shaman, Healer, Sage

*Soul Journeying**

*Yoga, Power & Spirit**

*Available from Hay House

All of the above are available at your local bookstore,
or may be ordered by visiting:

Hay House UK: www.hayhouse.co.uk
Hay House USA: www.hayhouse.com®
Hay House Australia: www.hayhouse.com.au
Hay House India: www.hayhouse.co.in

THE
WISDOM
WHEEL

A Mythic Journey through the Four Directions

ALBERTO VILLOLDO

HAY HOUSE

Carlsbad, California • New York City
London • Sydney • New Delhi

Published in the United Kingdom by:

Hay House UK Ltd, The Sixth Floor, Watson House,

54 Baker Street, London W1U 7BU

Tel: +44 (0)20 3927 7290; Fax: +44 (0)20 3927 7291; www.hayhouse.co.uk

Published in the United States of America by:

Hay House Inc., PO Box 5100, Carlsbad, CA 92018-5100

Tel: (1) 760 431 7695 or (800) 654 5126

Fax: (1) 760 431 6948 or (800) 650 5115; www.hayhouse.com

Published in Australia by:

Hay House Australia Ltd, 18/36 Ralph St, Alexandria NSW 2015

Tel: (61) 2 9669 4299; Fax: (61) 2 9669 4144; www.hayhouse.com.au

Published in India by:

Hay House Publishers India, Muskaan Complex, Plot No.3, B-2,

Vasant Kunj, New Delhi 110 070

Tel: (91) 11 4176 1620; Fax: (91) 11 4176 1630; www.hayhouse.co.in

Text © Alberto Villoldo, 2022

Project editor: Anna Cooperberg
Cover design: Jordan Wannemacher
Interior design: Nick C. Welch

The moral rights of the author have been asserted.

The information given in this book should not be treated as a substitute for professional medical advice; always consult a medical practitioner. Any use of information in this book is at the reader's discretion and risk. Neither the author nor the publisher can be held responsible for any loss, claim or damage arising out of the use, or misuse, of the suggestions made, the failure to take medical advice or for any material on third-party websites.

A catalogue record for this book is available from the British Library.

Tradepaper ISBN: 978-1-78817-579-1
Hardback ISBN: 978-1-4019-6280-7
E-book ISBN: 978-1-4019-6281-4

Audiobook ISBN: 978-1-4019-6282-1

To my wife Marcela,
and to our four children
Ian, Alexis, Kelly, and Meric

CONTENTS

INTRODUCTION

The teachings of the medicine wheel have existed in different forms throughout the world and been handed down through many generations of peoples since the beginning of time. This sacred map is an Indigenous spiritual technology for healing by connecting with Mother Earth, the energies of nature, and the cosmos.

The medicine wheel is also a *wisdom wheel:* think of it as an advanced tool or a process for working toward personal and planetary transformation. When you work with the wisdom wheel, you're healing not only your personal trauma—you're healing the trauma of all humanity and the Earth. You are interacting with actual energies and catalyzing a biological and spiritual evolution.

If we do what's required of us, we access the gifts of the wisdom wheel, freeing ourselves from predetermined fates and co-creating a new destiny. Then we can do more than merely fix the problems in our lives that drive us to vent, drink too much, and grouse about the people we blame for all our miseries. We can experience radical self-honesty. We will feel discomfort as we enter the growth process, but working with the wisdom wheel is key to transformation.

In doing the work of the wisdom wheel, we will interact with power animals, who are associated with each of the four directions and can help us. If we are willing to accept the wheel's challenge to further our evolution, we can awaken the master within: our potential to become a wisdom keeper, sage, and visionary. We can learn to help not just ourselves but all who are in need and even Mother Earth and all her creatures.

The wisdom wheel takes many forms. The one I use and teach is the one I learned over decades of working with the shamans of the Andes. The first time you pass through the cycle of the wisdom wheel is a journey of healing the self. As you go deeper, beyond healing from trauma and repairing the body, you discover your place around a sacred fire and take a seat that has been held for you since time immemorial: the seat of a shaman.

The Modern Shaman

Shamanism is the exercise of power, born of knowledge, with the goal of service to and compassion for all creation. Nowadays, shamanic wisdom that had been carefully guarded for centuries within Indigenous societies is being disseminated to a receptive world that urgently needs it. As a spiritual tradition rather than a religion, it adapts itself easily to the present. As a feminine tradition, it is sensitive to the needs of the vulnerable as well as the powerful.

Our goal—and challenge—as modern shamans is to do more than simply imitate the outer form of tradition. Instead, we must create new paradigms that incorporate the wisdom of science, both ancient and modern, and that are founded on the stewardship of the Earth and the health of the body and the village. The teachings of the Four Winds Society that I founded years ago and the medicine wheel within this book draw from the more than 25 years I spent working with shamans in the Andes, the Chimú and Mochica in Peru (known as Seers), and the Aymara of Lake Titicaca, as well as from my Western studies in psychology, neuroscience, and anthropology.

Years ago, to the amusement of my mentor Don Manuel Quispe, I would fret about getting everything absolutely "right." For example, when reciting a prayer, I'd become so caught up in my desire to be respectful of the wisdom ways that I'd get stuck in the details and reduce a ritual's meaning to a formula. When we remain too much in our heads, we miss feeling the shift into a new kind of perception that is sacred, integrative, and inclusive—the goal of all ceremonies.

It's important to honor and respect the traditions we learn from, making sure we are appreciating and understanding—without appropriating—the sacred practices of any Indigenous peoples. It's also important to know that your experience and interpretation are inherently valuable. For the shaman, the ultimate authority is Spirit, not words in a book or those spoken by priests.

The Call to Mastery

The shamans I studied with in the Andes say that if we master how we see ourselves, the events in our lives, and our relationships with others, we can start to dream a new world into being. Doing so requires that we work with the energies of the invisible realms, which have far more power over and influence on us than our will, intentions, or actions do.

The challenge is to avoid limiting our awareness to "me and mine." While it's natural to want to fix our personal problems, there is also deep healing work that urgently needs to be done on behalf of the *planet*. When we heal the Earth, we feel the repercussions in our own lives; as the fate of the Earth goes, so goes our fate.

As someone who teaches people to become modern shamanic practitioners, I know how easily a sense of self-importance can take over, corrupting motives and making aspirants obsess over the "right" way of doing things.

Knowledge can be seductive, feeding the mind at the expense of nourishing the soul. Students who become fascinated with their own interests instead of humbly doing the work of alleviating suffering and creating health are certain to fall under the spell of the ego.

The need for external validation makes us live according to old rules, whether or not they work for us. When this happens, we remain asleep to our destiny, clinging to our past, our reputations, and our beliefs that give us a strange sort of comfort. There is no greater enemy to mastery than the need to be "special." We must remain open to a wisdom far beyond that which the everyday mind can appreciate. The shaman strives to ascend to a higher level of wisdom and influence—and not for her* own sake but for the sake of all.

The Four Directions and Challenges

In this book, you will learn to work with the wisdom wheel and its four directions—South, West, North, and East—each of which is associated with an archetypal animal and a sacred journey. You will be invited to perform live ceremonies to embody the wisdom teachings, allowing you to bring in new energies: those of the four directions and the four power animals.

As you work your way through this ancient map, you will begin to see your life not as a continual, stressful battle but as part of a larger, mythic story shared by humans around the globe, a story of the Earth and her inhabitants. You will break free of the grip of ordinary time and causality. Enter the magic of synchronicity and begin to dream a new dream that will reshape your destiny—including the expression of

---

* Throughout this book, I will use the pronoun *she* to refer to an individual shaman so as to acknowledge both the feminine energy of Mother Earth and the overlooking of women healers throughout millennia. Shamans can, however, have any gender identity.

your DNA. This will allow you to create extraordinary health and to live and die differently from how your parents did.

The deeper work of the wisdom wheel is to encounter and engage the lessons of each of the directions, meeting the challenges so you can access their powerful healing energies. Each challenge involves sloughing off an old and dreary fate that blocks you from achieving your destiny and participating in the evolution to *homo luminous*, a new species of human ready to live harmoniously with the Earth and one another.

- **The wisdom challenge of the South,** of serpent, of shedding the fate of aging and dying that was preordained by your genetics and your lifestyle like the serpent sheds her skin. Pass the test and you step into a new future, one in which your life span and health span aren't determined by the past, allowing you to grow a new body and access the potential for the deepest kind of healing.

- **The wisdom challenge of the West,** of jaguar, of releasing yourself from an emotional and psychological fate that has you operating from primordial fear. Acquire jaguar wisdom and you can overcome your fear of your mortality and of losing your identity and memories that make you who you are. You can transcend betrayal in love and the old patterns of tragedy and suffering in romance. Then, like the jaguar, you become a courageous explorer. You discover possibilities hidden to you when you were ruled by fear, and your relationships are no longer characterized by hurt, betrayal, loss, and conflict.

- **The wisdom challenge of the North,** of hummingbird, of liberating yourself from confusing your job for the sacred work you came to do in this lifetime and the sage wisdom you sought to experience. Just like the hummingbird takes a mythic journey, you have the power to step into your destiny and contribute to harmony and peace on Earth. The gift of hummingbird wisdom is to experience stillness in flight, to become discerning and wise, and to cease exhausting yourself with unnecessary effort. Like the ancient sages, you learn to master time, tracking into the future to bring harmony to everyday life in the present, and master invisibility, practicing ayni, or reciprocity with nature and the ancestors.

- **The wisdom challenge of the East,** of eagle, of letting go of dogmatic beliefs and old constrictions on your spiritual nature. This requires you to resist the seduction of escaping into liminal consciousness to avoid the everyday work you are called to do, while rejecting the guilt-ridden ideas you have inherited from religion, science, and culture. Eagle wisdom frees you to become a visionary so you can consciously participate in the evolution into *homo luminous*, free from worn-out ideas that became solidified as teachings never to be questioned. This wisdom gift allows you to claim your extraordinary natural instincts and your spiritual destiny as a co-creator with the cosmos. Just as the eagle flies high enough in the sky to perceive the curvature of the Earth yet is able to spot a mouse below and descend to attend to the business of ordinary life, you can marry the spiritual and the mundane.

As a shaman, I am convinced that even if one person out of a thousand moves through the four challenges and passes the four tests to attain mastery, we can bring about new ways of living in harmony with one another and the Earth.

I like to think of the call to mastery as the experiment of *n-of-1*. *N* is the number of people in a research study. In science, you want to have *n* be as large as possible so that the results will be valid and reliable. Yet the great evolutionary experiment we are undergoing is happening at the level of each one of us. My experiment is called Alberto. If you do not take part in the evolution to *homo luminous,* you get to be part of the control group that does not experience transformation and remains a statistic. This is the unconscious mass of humanity that abuses the Earth, pollutes their bodies, and destroys their health. The future is not pretty for those who remain inside the normal range in the bell curve. Try to be an outlier and become a master of your destiny.

The wisdom wheel awakens our power to go beyond our perceived limitations. How we relate to ourselves and to other people will evolve. We will reduce conflict, suffering, and disappointment. Our self-importance and limited ideas and preconceptions will begin to disappear, freeing us to experience a lightness of being and even a greater sense of humor about ourselves and all that happens to us.

Right now, we need to dream into being a new reality, a new way of doing human life on our planet, more than ever. We need to awaken and become the masters we were meant to be. We need to break free from fate and step into new personal and collective destinies.

The Wisdom Keepers

To acquire mastery, it's very helpful to have a master who can guide you. I have been fortunate to have studied and worked with some great mentors—Don Manuel Quispe, Joan Halifax, Rolling Thunder, and Amchi Tenjing Bista—whom you will meet in this book. They challenged me to face my darkness and embrace my light. Their wisdom will, I hope, challenge you to dig deeply into what you believe you know or have mastered and be honest with yourself about the challenges you still need to meet.

Don Manuel Quispe

Don Manuel Quispe was a shaman from the mountains of Peru who continually challenged me to shift my perspective. His wry insults took me out of my self-absorbed slumber and fears into a deeper appreciation for new ways of seeing reality. Don Manuel had one foot in the world of his people's ancient tradition and the other in the modern world. He claimed that what you believe in your heart is exactly what you meet in the world. And he helped me see how the wisdom teachings of old could be applied to our everyday lives.

Don Manuel helped me understand ayni, which means having a right relationship with all beings as well as with the past and the future. He taught me that in practicing ayni, we should not come from fear but from reverence and awe. And we should welcome the destiny that ayni with the heavens offers us, no matter how uncomfortable it might feel at first.

Joan Halifax

Joan Halifax is a celebrated author, a Zen Buddhist teacher, the founder of the Project on Being with Dying, civil rights activist, LSD researcher, and anthropologist—and that's just a brief list of what she has done. In the 1970s, Joan was a resident scholar at the Esalen Institute, a retreat center that was formed out of the Human Potential Movement, in California. I met her when I was accompanying my friend and professor Dr. Stanley Krippner to lunch at her cottage overlooking the ocean in Big Sur.

"We have a sensory deprivation chamber in the basement," she told me that day. "You might want to try it out."

I had never been in one before, a warm water tank in complete darkness and filled with salt water that mimicked the composition of the water in the human body. It seemed like a great opportunity to take that tab of LSD I had been carrying in my wallet for weeks. Liquid sunshine in a piece of blotter paper!

Six hours and a lifetime later, I emerged from the tank wrinkled and reborn. I apologized for missing lunch, but that day marked a turning point for me. Joan was a medical anthropologist long before that term came into use, and inspired by her work, I would become one too after being changed by my experience in the sensory deprivation tank. I would travel to wild and sacred places, work with the shamans in the high Andes, and feel compelled to discover the ancient wisdom of traditional cultures in their places of origin. Joan's teachings and writings helped me understand that we are both part of the creative energy of the Earth and created by it.

Rolling Thunder (RT)

Rolling Thunder, or RT, as his friends called him, was an enigmatic spiritual leader who had earned his name because he could summon thunder and lightning, even in the middle of a desert drought. He was a Shoshone medicine man who lived on a run-down ranch in Carlin, Nevada. During the day, RT worked as a brakeman for the railroad, and in the evenings, he led sweat lodge ceremonies, tended to the sick, and received guests, including members of the Grateful Dead. In fact, I first met RT with my professor Stanley Krippner at Mickey Hart's ranch in California. At that time, Mickey was the percussionist for the Dead, and he and RT had developed a friendship (Mickey Hart would later release an album called *Rolling Thunder*).

RT was a controversial figure. Was he what he had claimed to be? Did he shift his identity as needed in order to do his work? He seemed to have the gift and power of shape-shifting, but was it all an illusion? Many times when I attended the fire ceremonies that he guided in the Arizona desert, he would disappear from the circle as we participants moved around in unison doing a snake dance. RT would then mysteriously reappear in the circle, seemingly emerging from nowhere. He was leading the ceremony, yet we kept losing track of him. "Invisibility," he said to me later, by way of explanation. "You should practice it more often."

I somehow knew that if I asked for more details, he would simply laugh at me. It always seemed that as soon as I felt I was getting a grasp on who he was and what RT was teaching me, he would make my head spin. RT often reminded me that the journey of awakening to our inner power has many twists and turns: we have to expect the unexpected and be flexible, holding on loosely to what we know instead of letting it calcify and become ideology.

Amchi Tenjing Bista

Amchi Tenjing Bista, or simply Amchi, which means "doctor" in the Tibetan language, is a master horseman and Buddhist priest. Amchi opened my eyes to the medicine of the Himalayas and his people's understanding of the connections among the mind, the emotions, and the body.

I got to see the many sides of Amchi during my expedition with him in Nepal: the Buddhist priest, the doctor, the teacher, and the horseman who looked like he was straight out of a cowboy movie. And above all, I admire that he is the founder of an orphanage that houses and educates homeless children. When the children grow into adulthood, he trains them in the art of Tibetan medicine. I have become a patron of his orphanage and help them where I can.

All of these wisdom keepers are (or were) imperfect individuals—flawed people, like you and me. Nevertheless, all of them achieved mastery in their own way, awakening their gifts to be more fully human and in service than they had imagined. All took what they learned and generously shared their gifts with others. I hope that in telling their stories and bringing my adventures with them to life on the page, I've done justice to their teachings.

What Will You Dream into Being?

Spirit is always attentive to our longings—that is, what we want for ourselves. However, we have to be willing to let go of our flawed beliefs about what's best for us, as this almost always involves trying to fix or repair a fate handed to us at our birth. Only when we start to awaken the master within can we step out of the nightmare we have been living in—the one scripted by fear and a scarcity mind-set that keeps us focused only on "me and mine" in the here and now.

We can do so much better. We can step into a destiny infused with meaning and purpose. We can become healers, explorers, sages, and visionaries, if only we will work with ancient technologies that burn away the old to make way for the new.

PART I

UNDERSTANDING

CHAPTER 1

IN SERVICE TO SOMETHING GREATER

The Kali Gandaki River, Nepal.

Dust.

Dust everywhere.

Dust in my eyes, in my ears, in my mouth; grit against my teeth.

Why do sacred journeys always involve hiking to a no-man's-land, into arid, windswept dust bowls like the one I encountered at the foot of the Himalayas?

Our destination was Lo Manthang, a tiny village that is all that remains of the ancient Kingdom of Lo, in Mustang, Northern Nepal, bordering Tibet and China. This is a protected region, only accessible with special permission from the government because of the precarious and complex relationship between Nepal and China.

To reach the village, one must walk or ride horses for twelve days over Himalayan passes. Guru Rinpoche followed this same route in the 8th century when he walked from India to Tibet, defeating demons and sorcerers as he traveled to bring Buddhism to a frontier land. In the years that followed his trek, a main trade route between Tibet and India was established along the banks of the Kali Gandaki River. We will be following Rinpoche's footsteps, meditating in his temples and caves.

As my throat protested with another round of coughing, I reminded myself of why I had come—to learn, to serve, and to connect with others I know to be dedicated to the same goals here in Nepal.

I remember being in the Nevada desert years ago, with dust devils whirling nearby, and thinking that spirituality is too often seen as comfort food. People want to feel better, to be happy. For life to be less hard. They want sacred medicine to be sweet, but it can be challenging in ways we don't expect. We are tested, shown our darkest fears and most terrible self-judgments. We have to heal and forgive those who hurt us and practice gratitude even when we don't understand why the lessons have to be so difficult.

Only then do we learn to find beauty everywhere we look. Only then do we see the beauty in the desert, the life that escaped our notice because it didn't appear in the forms we expected, causing us to focus on the seemingly endless sand.

Dust be damned. I was open to what I might discover on this journey.

I had been teaching shamanic energy medicine for many years when my wife, Marcela, and I accepted an invitation to travel to Nepal's border with Tibet in a pilgrimage to the Himalayas. An old acquaintance, Joan Halifax, was leading a team of physicians on a mission to bring Western and Tibetan medicine to remote villages along the Kali Gandaki River.

Joan made her mark as an anthropologist studying Cuban spiritualism and has authored numerous books on shamanism. Before she became a Buddhist teacher, we occasionally taught at the same conferences and retreats and shared tales and glasses of wine. This was to be her final journey to the land of Mustang in the Kingdom of Lo in Nepal. I was glad to hear that my friend Stephan, who had been Joan's doctor over the years and who founded the

Omega Institute in upstate New York, would be joining us. A few Western doctors and two amchis, or Tibetan physicians, plus a dozen or so Nepali guides and horsemen we'd hired to help us with camp, rounded out our team.

Marcela, who is a medicine woman, was looking forward to visiting ancient Buddhist sites along the Silk Road and communing with the energies there. We have explored more than one map of the afterlife with the Andean and Amazon shamans and were eager to learn about the teachings of sages in the Himalayas. In addition, I wanted to explore connections between geographically distant traditions that may have once shared a common origin.

In the field of molecular archaeology, there is growing evidence to support the idea that shamanic traditions of the Americas originated in Asia. Its practitioners have been tracing mutations in mitochondrial DNA that indicate that humanity left Africa tens of thousands of years ago. What sacred technologies became lost as we parted ways and fanned outward across the globe? The question has always nagged at me. It may be that all shamanic traditions share a common root in the same way that humanity shares a common mitochondrial Eve, our great-great-grandmother from Africa. I was convinced that the root may lie in shared experiences within the invisible realms.

The Tibetans and the shamans from the Americas are consummate cartographers of the invisible world. They mapped the journey beyond death in extraordinary detail. I was interested in comparing the maps to see where they shared common ground, where their shores coincided. And I was particularly interested in a teacher with great gifts known as Guru Rinpoche. We would be visiting his temples and meditation caves, powerful places where wisdom can be exchanged across time and brought back to the everyday realm of the five senses.

In the Himalayan region, people often undertake pilgrimages to discover the meaning of their lives and experience a deep healing. Such journeys require a willingness to let go of one's personal compass and navigate according to a new map. I was on this quest to the lands of the ancient Buddhists and shamans because I knew I would be humbled by the rugged terrain and advanced teachings. Here, I could rediscover the mastery that comes when we surrender our need to attain it.

Rechecking Our Maps

After the global events of 2020, we're more aware than ever of our interdependence with one another. Many of us who never questioned the assumptions with which we were raised—to be independent, to raise ourselves up by our bootstraps, to achieve at all costs—are now doing so. While some might be comfortable with reconsidering the customs they grew up with, others hesitate to question them. However, all of us can develop a deeper understanding of ourselves and our journeys if we explore wisdom ways that we never knew about.

When you work with maps or navigation apps, you realize that even when the landmarks depicted differ from what is on the map, the paths are the same. Throughout history, humans have spent a lot of time arguing about sacred teachings, the landmarks of religions—efforts that could have been spent on bringing about a better world for all, if only we had been encouraged to travel the roads to inner peace they offered.

You might find the ideas in this book disorienting. They might make you question who you are and what you know. Disorientation can be a good thing. When you have to recheck the maps you use to navigate your life, you can discover a new range of possibilities.

A Forgotten History

History is written by the conquerors, but we're starting to learn more about what elements of the wisdom traditions of the conquered became lost. This is causing us to question assumptions that we took for granted for many years.

Back in school, you might have read about the bravery of Europeans who "tamed" the "wild" lands of the American frontier and converted "savages" to Christianity in order to "save" them from their "sinful" beliefs and practices. It's important to explore these old assumptions because they have distorted the way many of us perceive the past and the Indigenous wisdom traditions.

Many traditional Native American cultures were grounded in the principles of honoring nature, serving the invisible world, being stewards of the land, and practicing diplomacy with their neighbors. Around the fire, people engaged in dialogue with one another. Some traveled many thousands of miles to visit the great cities of the Maya or the Pueblo, engaging in trade and sharing technologies and wisdom. Conflicts were easier to avoid when people came together in the market to talk through differences and remembered that everyone had something valuable to contribute.

With the arrival of the Europeans to the Americas came distinctly patriarchal traditions that were unfamiliar to the Indigenous people. The Europeans justified the exploitation of nature, greed, and the accumulation of wealth in the hands of the few at the expense of the many. Domination and subjugation of the native peoples were not just acceptable ideas; they were said to be commanded by God, particularly in North America, where the extermination of American Indians was widely practiced until the late 1800s. In the Andes, master shamans were persecuted, and the teachings they had handed down for generations seemed condemned to disappear forever. Cities were destroyed. Sacred texts were burned.

Shamanism went into hiding, but like the flame that suddenly appears in the moment you strike a match, it is present in its totality when you connect with this ancient tradition for the betterment of the world. While fragments of early writings leave gaps in our knowledge about the ancient sages, the Inca—the builders of cities in the clouds like Machu Picchu—also had an oral tradition and kept the embers of shamanism glowing, if dimly. They used the power of that light and its wisdom to create the largest known empire of the Western world to date. Along the way, they added their own unique fingerprint to the shamanic traditions before they returned to the embers and seemed to be lost for all time. In reality, the sacred teachings were only waiting for a gentle breeze for its flames to rise up once again to warm the hands and heart of the seeker.

As a young man, I took my first journey to the Peruvian Andes to meet the shamans and learn about their medicine, which led me to discover that my ideas about health were quite different from theirs. I had assumed my ways were superior. I had internalized what my people believed: that our wisdom ways were the truth, *the* way of understanding our relationship with the body and with Spirit. I believed that illnesses existed and were real. Cancer and heart disease and Alzheimer's certainly seemed terrifyingly real. I believed that health and longevity were the product of genetics and that DNA ruled your destiny. I believed that you should treat disease with medicine. Thanks to my mentors, I would lose these notions in time. I would discover that illnesses do not exist; sick people do. That your DNA determines only a small percentage of your health. That the largest percentage is determined by the quality of your relationship with the Earth and with Spirit (including your diet and lifestyle)—a relationship that the Andean peoples call ayni. I learned that if you create the conditions for health, disease often goes away on its own, with no medication required. I would learn many other lessons, which I will share in this book.

Drawn to shamanism, I was eager to find the wellspring where the waters of the timeless shamanic wisdom trickled out from the depths of the Earth. Or, to use a more appropriate metaphor, I wanted to find the source of the wool from which the threads that wove the cloth of the destiny and health of every person had been spun.

I was soon gathering the frayed strands of a magical tapestry of wisdom that was woven before the beginning of time. The Spanish Inquisition had done a grand job of persecuting the wisdom keepers while keeping the herbalists and midwives handy for when their people became sick or the populace they had enslaved were in need of healing from overwork and old age. The conquistadors knew the Americas' medicine was far superior to the leeches and bloodletting of plague-ravaged Europe. For millennia, medicine women had worked with the plants to access their healing powers.

To speak with Spirit through the plants that were an expression of this divine force would not have been met with the approval of the conquerors and their church of the male god. Spirit was up there, not down here; not numinous, as animists believe. Aware of the risk of seeming too powerful, the medicine women did not reveal the origins of their knowledge. They continued to heal the sick and deliver the babies of the conquerors, who were both frightened of and dependent on the medicine women's abilities. The shamans knew their deepest wisdom would have to remain underground until it was safe to reveal it again.

The Bigger Picture

The power a shaman engages in the invisible world is vastly different from the power that people seek in the visible mundane world to improve their lives. She is interested in entering a non-ordinary reality in the invisible realm to discover and engage with energies that affect and influence everyday life. She pursues an energy that is life-sustaining and prevents aging and disease so that she can bring healing and well-being to her community. In the East, this energy is known as prana, chi, or even the Tao. The Andean shamans know it as TI, and it forms part of the names of sacred places such as Lake Titicaca, the sea on top of the world, and the name Inti, the sun god. In this book, I will use the more familiar term *chi*, as in tai chi.

Chi is not the power to dominate or rule over others or nature, although nature indeed responds to the chi. It's not the power of money or material things, though those are available through it. It's not the power to defeat illness and old age, although health and longevity flow from it. It's the power to create and collaborate, to give birth to the new. The chi is to be used for the benefit of others, of all beings and the Earth. Otherwise, it will spoil and destroy you in the process. It must be shared so that all may thrive.

While a shaman can work on behalf of one individual, the most powerful shamans focus first on what they can do for Mother Earth. Only after they have considered Pachamama's needs do they focus on what they can do for their village and for all people. After that, they focus on what they can do for one person. This is the inverse of how most of us come to spiritual practice. Too often, we're so worried about fixing our individual situations or helping one person that we become oblivious to the bigger picture. When working on ourselves, we forget we're part of a cosmos far greater than ourselves that affects all of us and that we, in turn, can affect.

Mythologies That Shape Our Reality

To understand how a shaman finds her destiny in the service to all beings, we must examine the myths we may have taken for granted. Myths shape our perceptions, so the stories we carry within us have great power—especially when we aren't aware of them.

According to Joseph Campbell, author of *The Hero with a Thousand Faces*, myths offer clues to what we're capable of experiencing in our lives. They are metaphors for that which is transcendent and can't be known through thought alone. Myths provide pathways for connecting with the mysteries of who you are and who you might become. They inspire us to dream much bigger dreams and to see ourselves as minor players in the vastness of the cosmos but also potentially important actors in the grand scheme of things.

As Westerners, we are people of the *precept* (law). We address any difficult issues we have in our communities by coming up with rules and laws, enforcing them, and judging and punishing anyone who breaks them. Shamans are persons of the *percept* (perception). They change their perceptions to bring about changes in the realm of the everyday. They reframe situations and look at people—including themselves—from another angle to see what was previously hidden from their awareness. We can participate in our own evolution and transform our experiences if we master the art of shifting our perceptions.

In the West, we say that perception occurs inside the brain as we try to make sense of what we are experiencing. The brain interprets signals sent to it from the body's sensory systems. The eye interprets signals from the world outside of us in the form of photons (units of light) that strike the retina and get carried by the optic nerve to the visual cortex in the back of the brain. That's our scientific understanding of sight—yet perception involves both what we see and how we think about or understand it. Everything that we perceive is a projection of an internal map of reality we carry within us—in our mind and in our energy field.

Shamans say vision can flow in the opposite direction: rather than interpreting what the eye sees, the mind can create it. I'm not talking about a hallucination. When you can perceive the invisible world, where things exist in potential before taking form, you can project those ideas into the world of the senses. You can change the map of reality that you carry within you, and this changes the reality you experience when you are going about your everyday activities. The ancient sages called this "dreaming the world into being." They believed that seeing—or sight—is the act of perceiving reality, while vision is the act of co-creating it.

Personal Energy

To co-create reality requires fuel—chi. A shaman channels power from outside her own body, sourcing it from the field of energy shared by the cosmos. If she were sourcing it from her own field of energy, the work would be exhausting.

Each of us has only so much personal energy for fueling a vision that can affect everyday reality. If you've heard of the Law of Attraction or manifestation and wondered why it didn't seem to work for you, the problem may have been that you were drawing solely on the power of your wishing and intention rather than on chi. On an individual level, working with the chi can help a shaman bring about spontaneous healing in a person who is ill. On a collective level, shamans can work together to create abundance, health, and well-being in their communities.

The Andean shamans' perception of the life force is very different from that held by Westerners. Religious teachings tell us that the life force was created by God and is present in humans, plants, and animals until they die. Shamans are animists: they would say the life force, the chi, is everywhere. Access it, and you can draw beneficial life energies into your being and release what you have decided you don't need anymore. This is similar to what we do every day with the food we eat. But it works at other levels too.

The jaguar was my power animal when I was a young man, and this aspect of the life force taught me to find my own path instead of unquestioningly following the one I was expected to follow: the one that would make my family happy and proud. When I became a father, I encountered a wolf while doing shamanic journeying and understood that I needed a new wisdom to shift into my new role. I had to embody the leader of a pack who is looking out for those who are in need of protection, and who is always loyal to the pack yet roams far from it at times. The jaguar had served me well and would remain with me for the rest of my days, but I was now in need of wolf energy and wisdom.

Assistance from Invisible Realms

Shamans know that spiritual assistance from the invisible realm is always available to us. There are luminous beings that are ready to midwife the dying into the realm after death and help the living embody wisdom and healing. The problem is that as a result of our greed, the mists between the visible and invisible worlds have become very thick. Our desire to be in control, to have the power to change situations we don't like, is an obstacle if we want to cross the bridge to reach the invisible worlds where magic can happen.

The Andean shamans call the visible realm the "middle world." It exists between two invisible realms, the lower world and the upper world. In the lower world, we can access the ancient wisdom of the ancestors and heal the past. In the upper world, we can interact with the future, our becoming, and guides who want to help us get on a path to a tomorrow better than the one we seem fated to experience. The middle world is the realm of the present, ordinary experiences from interacting with neighbors to watching the first buds on the trees open in the springtime to drinking a cup of tea.

When a shaman operates with integrity and is driven by vision informed and fueled by the chi rather than personal desire or a sense of scarcity and fear, knowledge and power recognize her and begin to stalk her relentlessly. The call to be a shaman, to participate in this work of serving something greater than yourself, can feel intense.

Those who have traveled through the mist into the invisible realms offer us much wisdom and guidance. Students look to mentors who can teach them the ancient ways and may initiate them into a lineage of wisdom keepers. (Note that a mentor is important but not essential.) Shamans also learn from nature herself. That's because ours is a living universe, and nature feels the longing of one who searches with sincerity for wisdom and assistance.

The shaman can learn from the wind, the trees, the rivers, the rain, and the lightning bolt, but this will not happen if we believe that we are here to dominate or tame nature for our own purposes. We are obligated both to protect the Earth and to recognize that we are always intertwined with her. Nature will only reveal her secrets when we are willing to become her keepers. Then the shaman can meet power directly, embrace it, and claim it while developing an active dialogue with the cosmos. This is called ayni, or reciprocity, and it is a core principle in shamanism: give and you will receive.

Spirit Helpers

Often, it is spirit helpers from the other side that assist with or even do the healing work for the shaman, performing interventions including "surgeries," removing heavy and toxic energies, and helping the souls of the dead return to centers of healing in the spirit world. You can witness amazing things when you can perceive the world, and the space between the worlds, differently.

That said, I know that the notion of invisible helpers can be unsettling for some in the West. I remember being in the Amazon rain forest once and speaking with a native healer, telling him that it's always good to wash a wound or a cut, especially in the jungle, as it is full of invisible life.

"You mean spirits," he said.

"No," I said, "I mean microbes. Invisible creatures that want to eat you and reproduce inside you."

"Where are they? I haven't seen them. How do you know they exist?" he asked. He needed to see to believe. These minute critters that can make us very sick are visible under a microscope, but there is no spirit-scope yet that will make the spirit world visible to the naked eye. Only when you develop the shaman's way of seeing do you truly understand that the cosmos is full of life, both visible and invisible, and that it's possible to engage luminous beings who want to assist you.

In the next chapter, you will learn how to cleanse and balance your energy system. You will learn how to invite a power animal into your energy body; it will help you, serve as your ally, and reset your natural instincts. The way of the shaman is paved with assistance, if only you ask for it.

CHAPTER 2

OUR ENERGETIC MAKEUP

Carol Dunham called me over to show me a gadget she had just picked up: an ultraviolet light pen for sterilizing drinking water. I glanced into the metal cup in her hand, full of a cloudy liquid that looked like milk of magnesia but which I know is particle-filled water.

Carol is an American anthropologist who earned her Ph.D. at Princeton and has lived for years in Mongolia and Nepal, becoming an expert on ancient Buddhism. I admire her willingness to dive deep into her work, even moving her family to the steppes of Mongolia so she could continue her research on the divine feminine in Buddhism. Years of living in far-flung regions seem to have taught her all sorts of ways for making do with what you have.

I watched Carol down half of the liquid, and then she offered me the rest. "No, thanks," I say.

"Suit yourself." She shrugged and walked away before I had a chance to finish what I meant to say: that I'd spent far too long being sick in the jungles and had no interest in starting our high-altitude trek with an upset stomach and gastrointestinal

distress. I knew of the power of UV light to kill microbes but pre-ferred my water free of floating particles—and I knew Carol's gut flora was accustomed to the microbial wildlife of the Himalayas.

Just a few years ago, I had been brought to the brink of death, so exhausted I could barely move. Multiple types of viruses and par-asites had transformed my gut microbiome into a tangled mess of unwanted visitors who had merrily moved in and trashed the place. My liver was threatening to quit on me. I could get on a transplant list, but I wondered, Is this really what the last chapter of my life will be defined by? *Here, I had been teaching people about energy medicine and shamanic wisdom and healing practices for years. I'd even co-written a book with David Perlmutter, M.D., on the neuro-science of enlightenment: clearing out the toxins that reduce brain function to prepare yourself for higher states of consciousness. I'd done all this only to face a formidable set of health problems that would take my full attention for more than two years.*

I changed my diet. I dutifully took the medicines nature offered me—supplements and probiotics but also time in the nat-ural world. There, I was able to reconnect with the quantum field and nourish myself, reinvigorating the energy centers in my body and beginning to repair the fuel factories in my cells. There was much work to do, and at times I felt I wouldn't make it, but I'd come through and reclaimed my health. Now I was trusting that my body could carry me through high-altitude challenges on a trek that had great meaning for me.

My gut and the environment had declared a truce, but I con-tinued to be cautious about new skirmishes. And I had discov-ered that the health of my gut and the 90 trillion cells that make up my microbiome was influenced by the health of my second chakra, that spinning vortex of light above the navel that the med-ical Chi-Kung practitioners consider the storehouse of chi.

Modern physics helps us understand how all of creation works together in its intricate and elegant dance of life— including at the micro and macro levels of particles and waves of light and of galaxies, black holes, and solar systems. However, it's shamanic wisdom that helps us experience the workings of creation that are invisible to and as yet not understood by our science.

Understanding our energetic makeup and how it interacts with the field of energy shared by all of life requires letting go of two things: old ideas about our separateness and any myths about being ejected from the Garden of Eden. Shamans know that we are unified with the whole, woven together into the tapestry of life. When we recognize the relationship we have with the field and the energetic gifts it has to offer us, we empower ourselves to claim those gifts and transform ourselves and our lives. Unlike in other traditions, shamanic wisdom teaches us that we never left the Garden. If we shift our perception, we can recognize that and interact effectively with the energy field that we are part of and influence it in ways that help us thrive.

Electrons and the Field

In the early 20th century, physicists discovered that the electron has both a particle state and a field state. In fact, the electron is a wave that will collapse into a particle when you attempt to measure its position. When you fire an electron at a steel plate with a hole in it, the electron will pass through it like a bullet, so obviously, it has to be a particle. If the steel plate has three slits in it instead of a hole, the electron will pass through all three like an ocean wave washing its way through a wooden fence, so obviously, it has to be a wave. Although scientists were initially reluctant to recognize that the electron had both a field state and a particle state, they eventually came around to accepting this strange notion.

The behavior of electrons can be seen as a metaphor: it suggests that every human being has a particle state (a body) and a field state (which we'll call the *energy body*). Your energy body is part of the quantum field into which all reality is woven, including the chair you're sitting on, the air that you're inhaling and exhaling in exchange with plants, the land and the sea, the dragonflies and the elephants, the sky and the stars. The separation between you and everything else is a trick of the mind.

When you practice shamanic healing, you are working with energy—around you and within you—to upgrade the quality of your energy body. This field of energy is infused with wisdom. This means that what happens outside of you affects what happens inside of you, and what happens inside of you affects your body and what goes on in your world. What you vibrate, you create.

All living beings have a nervous system and an energy field that envelops them, an electromagnetic field created by electrons flowing through long nerves. This energy field interacts with the quantum field of the cosmos. But what is this field we are woven into? The language of physics helps us understand what has been described in largely esoteric terms: *emptiness* by the Buddhists and *ether* by the European mystics. For many in the West, the scientific concept of a quantum field can seem less "out there" and more real than the concept of a void, ether, or universal consciousness. But shamans will tell you that within the field exists not just energy but consciousness—the consciousness of Spirit, which is characterized by love and wisdom.

Mastery of Invisible Fields

Ninety-five percent of reality is happening in the invisible world of energy, not in front of our eyes. You and I see only about 1 percent of all light. Nearly 95 percent of the universe's mass is made up of material that scientists cannot observe or measure. This "dark matter" doesn't emit light or energy, but it's there.

The authority of the shaman comes from a personal experience of the unseen. The shaman knows the way to and from the invisible spirit realm and how to engage with and affect what she finds there. She becomes a master of both worlds: the world of form and the world of formlessness, the realm of matter and the realm of energy. Shamans travel through this in-between space, crossing over from the visible world to the invisible one so they can bring change to the physical world, helping people and communities to heal, babies to be born, elders to die, and ideas to come to life.

The ancient sages of the Americas and the Himalayas were masters at working with the field and consummate cartographers of the invisible world. The fact that you could not measure it, see it, or make accurate predictions about it—the fact that it didn't behave according to how you thought it should—did not mean that you could not experience it. Like dark matter, this invisible world doesn't neatly conform to the expectations and needs of scientific researchers. In mapping these hidden realms, the sages learned of the journey beyond death into infinity and the ultimate destiny of souls.

To explore the invisible world, shamans had to learn a unique form of perception known as the shaman's way of seeing: the *kawak,* in the Andean language. (*Kawak* means "seer" or "to see.") We know from Heisenberg's uncertainty principle that by observing a particle, the observer influences its position. Similarly, the kawak is the observer affecting physical reality. The more powerful the shaman, the better able she is to bring what has only been imagined into form, whether it's the health of an individual or even of a community. Kawaks recognize the dynamic nature of reality and consciously work with it to enact change. Some shamans use sacred plants to shift their consciousness and awaken their kawak ability, but the more an individual does shamanic work, the easier it is to make this shift without any help from the plants Mother Earth provided so that we, her children, could more easily communicate with her.

While Western (Judeo-Christian) worship is a tradition of prayer and Eastern spiritual practice has contemplation as its cornerstone, shamanism is a practice of active engagement with the powers of nature. That engagement involves interacting with life's energy fields to transform them.

The Chakras, or "Wheels of Life"

Known as "wheels of life," chakras are centers within the body's energy field. Many are familiar with them through descriptions from the Hindu and Tibetan traditions, but chakras are universal: these energy centers are found in every shamanic culture, just as mathematics is universal even though it was sages in the Arab world who discovered the concept of zero and algebra. Wheels of spinning energy, chakras were seen as magical centers where the body would draw in life force, what is called chi or prana, from the natural world.

Chakras connect the cells and tissues of the body to our personal energy field and the quantum field. They transform biophotons, which contain information from the quantum field, into electrical and hormonal signals essential for our health and well-being. This information is provided by the forest, the oceans, and the desert canyons, as well as by the sun. In fact, all the energy our bodies take in ultimately originates from the sun. When we sit around the fire at night, the flames are releasing sunlight that the branches and trunk of that tree stored as the Earth circumnavigated the sun.

We are fed and informed by the light entering through our chakras. Through these energy centers, we learn about the health of our local ecosystem, which informs our own health. If the Earth is sick around us, we receive signals of the ills that Mother Earth is experiencing.

When clear, a chakra shines with one of the seven colors of the rainbow. But our chakras are influenced by our emotions, especially trauma. Life events that hurt us emotionally cause our chakras to become dull, dimming our light; they can make our entire world seem dark. Instead of tapping into our courage or creativity, we put our focus on survival and start seeing threats all around us, worrying about problems when we could be dreaming up solutions. When the chakras have been damaged by emotional trauma, our primitive brain, which focuses on the four Fs—feeding, fighting, fearing, and fornicating—dominates the way we feel. We lack the power to break out of that limited mind-set. Detoxifying our chakras can free us, opening up our minds and awakening us to our potential. Therefore, the task of the shaman is to clear each chakra as well as possible and infuse it with the pure, translucent energy of Spirit.

How Information Is Stored within Our Chakras

Because the shamanic traditions in the Americas share common roots with the traditions in the Himalayas, it's not surprising that they share similar descriptions of the landscape of the world of energy. The Tibetans recognize five chakras, as do the shamans of the Andes, who identify five energy "systems" in the body. The Hindu traditions describe seven chakras. Because the seven-chakra system is the most well-known, we'll be working with that one. This seven-chakra system corresponds to our physiology and coincides with seven major endocrine glands and nerve plexuses in the body. The chakras are located where endocrine glands and a nerve bundle (a nerve plexus) coincide—a meeting of the central nervous and hormonal systems.

When you work with a chakra, you are directly influencing these two communication systems in the body. The nervous system uses electrical signals traveling along nerves to convey information, while the hormonal system employs chemical messengers. You might think of the electrical system as digital because it communicates at the speed of light, while hormones, the chemical messengers, are analog—very slow by comparison.

The ancient sages did not know the anatomy of the chakra system. They were able to describe only the vortex, or "wheel," they perceived. To them, a chakra was like an organ that served a key function in the energy body.

I like to think of a chakra like a hard drive that holds information—the story of a person's life. The memory of all our trauma and tragic stories and the details of how we suffered or hurt others—all the high-emotional-voltage events in our lives—are recorded in a chakra. If you have ever been surprised by some file hidden deep in your hard drive that you thought you deleted but hadn't, you can understand how memories can get deeply lodged inside one of your energy wheels. Each chakra has a theme and a period of time from your life associated with it: the stories of your first seven years of life are in the first, the stories of your next seven years in the second, and so forth, up to the seventh chakra at the crown of your head. When we arrive at that level, we have reached spiritual maturity.

The chakras hold the codes for a fate that has been selected for us that preordains our future health, happiness, search for meaning in life—and ultimately, our union with the divine. These fates are influenced by our genetic inheritance, our upbringing, and our experiences in this life. We can free ourselves from these fates if we commit to deeply cleaning our energy centers by harmonizing our chakras often and doing the work of the wisdom wheel.

The Seven-Chakra System

The first chakra is located at the base of the spine. Also known as the root chakra, it holds the fate of your physical health, as well as your power to survive illness, disease, and the ravages of aging. Here is where you can defy the statistics about the death you are most likely to experience.

This chakra is the abode of the serpent, which holds both the gift of healing and the Kundalini, the force of your passion.

The second chakra is located two fingers down from the belly button, above the pubic bone. Also known as the sacral chakra, this is where your emotional fate is encoded. Here you experience your power to embrace life and to find intimacy, allowing yourself to be vulnerable as you explore emotions and feelings outside of what your family has expected you to pursue. This center can predispose you to suffer from fatigue, low energy, helplessness, and hopelessness.

This chakra is the abode of the jaguar and its medicine of immortality and freedom from fear.

The third chakra is located at the solar plexus. This chakra holds the fate of trying to find your life's work through what you do rather than who you are and who you could become. Unless you release yourself from it, this fate will ensure that you take the long route to discover your mission and purpose in the world. This chakra holds the fate of your professional destiny: how you will find your true work, not just a job to pay the bills.

The solar plexus chakra is the abode of the humming-bird and its medicine of stillness in flight, of being present with what's happening instead of distracting yourself and wasting your energy on fruitless activities.

The fourth chakra is located at the heart. This chakra holds the fate of your experience of God and the divine. It is the place of the sacred heart and the boundless love of creation. And it is the center of mystical revelation and communication of pure inspiration, where you can become a clear conduit for Spirit's love and wisdom.

The heart chakra is the abode of the eagle and its medicine of clear sight of your infinite destiny that lies beyond the fates you have inherited.

The fifth chakra is located at the hollow of the throat. This chakra is where you can shed old voices, even voices of the wisdom teachers who seem to have guided you well, and claim your power to express yourself authentically and effectively in new ways. This work is essential for stepping into your destiny at this new stage in human evolution.

The sixth chakra is located on the center of the forehead between the eyes. Sometimes known as the third eye chakra, this is where you experience your relationship with the quantum field as reciprocal and where you can participate fully in harmonious co-creation with it.

The seventh chakra is located on top of the head and is the center of pure being and bliss where you connect to your divine destiny and the great mystery. The crown chakra is where you can experience freedom from all your limited ideas about who you are, for this is the realm of pure spirit, where you experience the void in which you shed your selfness and open to experiencing oneness with the quantum field. Then you are liberated from the fate of missing the forest for the trees, of failing to see the hand of Spirit everywhere, of living the rest of your life cast out of paradise with no hope of return or redemption.

The chakras contain the fate that has been selected for us by our ancestors and our early life traumas. In these energy centers, we hold unconscious beliefs about the world, which our experiences will inevitably prove true. The problem is not with the chakra, which is the hardware within the energy body, but with the software: the instructions the chakras are programmed with. Once we upload version 2.0 of the human software, we can enlist their amazing power. With upgraded instructions, our chakras will guide us to discover how to transform our job into our life's work—or do our life's work regardless of the jobs we have. We can find love and intimacy based on trust. And once the old fate has been overwritten, we will be able to see through the bias and the dogma of our upbringings—or our resistance to anything mystical or spiritual—and authentically experience the divine.

In later chapters, you will learn how to combust the fates held by each of your chakras in a holy fire so that you become available to your destiny and calling. However, before you begin to combust the fates associated with each chakra, you must verify they are spinning properly and balance them if they're not. This will help you remove the more recent and "surface" debris that has settled in the chakra. Chakra cleansing and balancing, along with eating healthfully and spending time outdoors in nature, make it easier to upgrade your energy body and be able to take in powerful healing energies that can help you protect your health and well-being.

Clearing and Balancing Your Chakras

Cleansing and balancing the chakras removes emotional debris: feelings of anger, fear, or despair. We can balance the chakras with each other, much like a piano tuner uses a tuning fork to find middle C and then tunes the rest of the piano to that note. We begin by tuning the heart chakra, our energetic equivalent to middle C. And just as there are seven notes in the musical scale, each tuned to a different frequency, there are seven colors or frequencies to the seven chakras.

The heart is the great drummer of the body, the great rhythm keeper that makes sure the band plays harmoniously. Thus, we tune each chakra to the heart center. We also tune it to the heart of Mother Earth so that we are in harmony with her. In the East, the heartbeat of the Earth is said to be the sound of the sacred syllable *om* (or *aum*). When tuning your chakras, you might want to take a deep breath and hum the syllable *ommmmmm* during the process—or you might imagine that you can hear or feel the heartbeat of Mother Earth.

To tune her heart chakra, the shaman first opens her wiracocha (a Quechua word meaning "the source of the Sacred" or "the supreme deity")—an energy center above the head that has been pictured in cultures around the world as a halo or an aura. If you're a master shaman, your wiracocha shines like a radiant sun, bathing you in your light and wisdom.

The wiracocha is what the Europeans called the soul. While your conflicting emotions and unhealed trauma can dim the light of your wiracocha, the wiracocha itself always remains pure in much the same way that clouds can dim the light of the sun while the sun itself remains radiant.

When we leave the physical body at death, what is left is our wiracocha, our energy body that has been freed from its cells, organs, and tissues. And while our physical body allows us to inhabit and travel through the middle world of our everyday experiences, the wiracocha allows us to travel and visit the lower and upper worlds freely.

You do not have to die to experience your wiracocha because you are your wiracocha, which has organized and created a physical body for you to inhabit in this lifetime. You also experience your wiracocha during your dreams, for it is the dreamer. It takes spirit flights: the out-of-body experiences that you hear about in shamanic lore. Tales of shamans temporarily taking leave of their bodies to travel to another realm and perhaps even take another form—shape-shifting—are tales about their wiracocha, which can "astral travel."

The wiracocha exists in many worlds, which overlap like circles. On one side exists the material world of particles, of the body and brain. On the other is the quantum field. I imagine the wiracocha like the equal sign in Einstein's formula $E = mc^2$, equating energy and matter. While we are alive, the wiracocha extends even farther—down into the Earth, like a tree stretching its roots deep into the soil, allowing us to sense the pulse of the Mother. Like an infant lying on her mother's chest being comforted by her mother's heartbeat, the shaman allows herself to be held and embraced by the love of Mother Earth, and her energy body and her heart begin to pulse to this rhythm. This attunement results in an inseparable connection to nature, as you are always held by the Mother. Whether in a parking lot in a crowded mall or by the edge of the river in the Amazon, you are always one with the Mother and with nature.

Nature balances your wiracocha, which in turn balances and maintains the health of the physical body. Remember that the chakras give messages to the endocrine and central nervous systems, the two main communications systems in the body. A shaman can strengthen her physical body by balancing the chakras and feeding them with the pure chi from nature. While the physical body requires physical food, the energy body requires chi, its essential nourishment. Chi enters into the chakra system, and through your nervous system and your hormones, it can balance your body at a cellular level. I like to think of the chi as the milk from our Mother Earth that nourishes and sustains us throughout our lives, especially in our later years.

Exercise: Testing, Balancing, and Cleansing the Chakras

To balance your chakras, stand up and place your left hand at the base of your spine and hold your right hand over the front of your body, feeling (or sensing) for the first chakra. You will feel it spinning lazily in a clockwise direction. When trying to feel for a chakra, keep in mind that the locations of these funnel-like energy centers are approximate. Like a whirlwind extending one or two inches outside your body, a chakra can shift position while the narrow tip of its funnel remains anchored to an endocrine gland and nerve plexus along your spine.

Next, backwash the first chakra: this means to spin it counterclockwise, removing and flicking off any sticky energies you find. To me, this often feels like I'm removing cobwebs or cotton candy from the bowl of the chakra. Occasionally I might find the memory of an old trauma there, represented by a symbol like a knife or an arrow that suggests a wound or a betrayal. Remember that you are in the world of symbols here, not the literal physical realm. Remove and flick off whatever you find that does not belong in that chakra—nothing but energy belongs there.

Next, tap your first chakra, and using your fingers, spin the chakra clockwise. The chakra will tune itself to your own heart, which you tune to the heartbeat of Mother Earth by repeating to yourself the syllable *om* or imagining sinking a taproot deep into the womb of Mother Earth.

Repeat this process with every one of the chakras, working your way up to the seventh at the crown of the head. When you're finished, hover your hand over each of these energy centers to make sure that all are spinning smoothly in a clockwise direction.

If you would like to perform a cleansing and tuning on a loved one or client, you must obtain permission first. Suppose you can't ask a person directly because of their physical state (for example, they are comatose), psychological state (for example, they are in a state of confusion), or their physical separation from you. In that case, visualize the person next to you and use this body wisdom technique to find the answer to the question "Is this a good time for me to perform a chakra tuning on _____?"

If you're like many in the West, you aren't used to thinking about or actually working with your energy body and its interaction with the quantum field. Before you do so in the fire ceremonies in Part II of this book, there is one more type of energy you need to know about. It is that of the divine feminine, and it has been missing from the Western psyche, thereby causing disharmony, for too long.

CHAPTER 3

RECLAIMING THE DIVINE FEMININE

I met up with Joan Halifax a few minutes after breakfast. I hadn't seen her in years but found her still brilliant, fearless, and unstoppable. I've always been moved by what she wrote in her book The Fruitful Darkness: *"Some of us are drawn to mountains the way the moon draws the tide. Both the great forests and the mountains live in my bones. They have taught me, humbled me, purified me, and changed me."[1]*

Joan is 75 years old and still riding horses through the Himalayas, but she had decided that this was going to be her last journey to the wilds of Mustang. "Just a group of friends on a medical expedition following the footsteps of Guru Rinpoche" was how she put it.

Joan led us out of the inn's dining hall and onto the main street in Kagbeni, promising a one-kilometer walk to the edge of town, where Amchi Tenjing Bista would be meeting us with horses from Mustang. When we arrived at the edge of town and the banks of the Kali Gandaki, I braced myself for the cold shock of fording the river—no more than eight inches deep at this spot. As we reached the other side of the stream, we faced a bigger problem than wet socks and pants: no horses, no Amchi Bista. We waited a bit, peering into the distance, and then realized we would have to occupy ourselves for a day or so.

Joan pointed to a spot halfway up the mountain to the right of us. "There's a Bön Buddhist monastery up there. We can camp in its courtyard. The horses will probably arrive tomorrow morning." Her confidence in that last point was greater than mine, but I felt it best to trust that the details would sort themselves out without effort on our part.

We were at an altitude of 3,000 meters, nearly 10,000 feet, and the monastery looked to be another 500 meters of vertical ascent. I took some deep breaths. It was a climb to be taken slowly if one isn't yet acclimated to the altitude—and I wasn't.

Hours later, we arrived—panting and disheveled, top layers of clothing soaked with sweat and shed after our trek along the steep trails. Joan explained that the dilapidated mud buildings we were looking at were part of a Bön monastery belonging to the old Tibetan shamanic religion, the only remaining one in the area. Other Buddhist sects had relentlessly persecuted practitioners during the 7th and 8th centuries. Many had fled to Mongolia and China. Only recently had the Dalai Lama recognized the Bön as a legitimate school of Buddhism.

At one time, there may have been a cadre of monks and nuns living here, but the Bön are the poorest of the Buddhist orders— now the mud-and-stone walls are crumbling in areas while nearby stands what looks like a collection of deserted huts. The place is so run-down, I felt certain no life was left in it, but Joan said that it is still in use.

The buildings' artwork is breathtaking, terrifying, and extraordinarily enchanting. The paintings of Sipe Gyalmo on the walls of the meditation hall depict her as exquisitely ferocious. She rides sidesaddle on a braying mule, barreling down the mountain enveloped in flames, her bare chest showing her breasts hanging by her waist, the sword drawn in her right hand ready to cut off heads, the brain of a devotee clutched in her left.

Damn, *I thought*. I like this vision of the sacred feminine!

The Bön Buddhists revere a Great Mother deity who is both a powerful protector and a fierce destroyer. The depictions and stories of her remind me of the Amazon shamans' tales of the female jaguar, a protective force that teaches us not to be afraid of death and destruction, for these are unavoidable parts of the cycle of life. The jaguar fearlessly glides into the waters of the Amazon and adeptly navigates the river's currents. She shields her cubs from harm and will not hesitate to kill to protect and provide for them.

In the Andean tradition, shamans call the organizing principle in the universe Illa Tici Viracocha: the one who is everywhere and in everything. But somehow, the Sun Father and Earth Mother gave way to the Father and the Son in the traditions of the conquerors of North and South America. Around the world, the power of the feminine can get lost in stories about goddesses serving male deities. They're often relegated to secondary or tertiary characters. Could that have to do with the gender of the keepers of these tales?

With such mythologies guiding us, we shouldn't be surprised that we no longer honor both our mother and our father, the masculine and feminine, equally.

"It's Complicated"

Sipe Gyalmo, the Bön deity whose name means "queen of the universe," is a fierce protector who is also compassionate and wise and offers her powers to those who honor her. The divine feminine has many faces, but because she has been driven underground in cultures around the world, we have only hints about the extent of her powers. The story I told of the conquistadors tolerating the women healers who were able to serve the needs of sick and wounded Europeans has been echoed elsewhere: As long as the medicine women demonstrated that they knew their place in the hierarchy of power, they were allowed to prosper in small ways. But if they showed their ferocity, displayed a wisdom greater than those of the men in power, or defied rules written by the community's male leaders, they usually paid a steep price. We see this in the stories from Europe where women were tortured and killed for being "witches"—meaning they followed an Indigenous spiritual tradition that honored the feminine aspect of divine power. The patriarchal diminishing of women and exalting of men can even be felt today, a remnant of the old myths that shape our perceptions in ways we don't even recognize.

Mother Earth and Father Sky do not have to be at war with each other. The way to mastery and wisdom requires that we get them to reconcile.

New Mythologies

In this book, you will learn to work with the wisdom wheel and its four directions—a map unique to Andean shamanism—each of which is associated with an archetypal animal and a sacred journey. The wheel is a tool for healings and transformations that you are able to midwife with the help of Mother Earth, who is protective and loving but who will challenge you to your core. You will at times feel nurtured by her; other times, you will hear her ferocious roar and quake at her terrifying power. Transformation is not always a gentle, easy process.

Earlier, I said that you would need to face four wisdom challenges to release yourself from four fates and achieve their gifts: new destinies offered by the wisdom wheel and the directions of South, the serpent; the West, the jaguar;

the North, the hummingbird; and the East, the eagle. You'll be learning skills that can help you understand how to awaken the master within who has the potential to evolve into *homo luminous*. To enjoy the new destinies, you will have to embrace some new mythologies.

In ancient times, the medicine women of the community drew upon the information in the quantum field by listening to the plants, which spoke to them and explained how to use their healing powers. The flowers and herbs offered their wisdom, and in return, the medicine women offered gratitude and respect to Mother Earth. The relationship between the healers and Earth was reciprocal—it was one of ayni: of right relationship. It was one of collaboration, not domination.

The wisdom of the medicine women went beyond knowing how to heal the body's ailments, and it was so powerful that the ancients knew it would have to remain secret until it was safe to reveal it again. It allowed those who sought healing to free themselves of more than just pathogens or symptoms of an illness. It allowed them to grow a new body that aged, healed, and died differently—or that perhaps never perished. And it allowed them, most importantly, to be freed of culturally planted beliefs that likely shaped their ideas and emotional reactions.

In working with the wisdom wheel and the roots of our limitations, we become able to choose our destiny, one in which we're liberated from our genetic legacy, our fears about death and loss, our confusion about the work we are meant to do in this lifetime, and our dogma related to religion and science that keeps us from having our own spiritual experiences. We can ditch the old mythologies at last.

The Divine Within and Around Us

Years ago, my mentor Don Manuel Quispe asked me about the Western notions about God. We had spent the night at Moray, camping at an ancient agricultural temple and laboratory where the Inca bred and crossbred their wisdom and their corn. Now we were hiking back to our vehicles, ascending a steep incline. I found it difficult to have a conversation as I pushed forward and had to stop frequently to draw in a deep breath of mountain air to keep from becoming too light-headed. Well acclimated to these heights and sure-footed despite his advanced age, Don Manuel did not miss a step as I tried to keep up with his sharp mind.

"Where is this God of yours located?"

"In heaven," I replied.

"So he is not here on Earth?" he asked.

"No," I said. "The God I learned about left his people on Earth to fend for themselves and occasionally destroyed them when they misbehaved, creating a flood or another cataclysm. He watches from afar. Our job is to emulate him. Not by being destructive. By taking care of the world he created. Although we screwed up at the beginning in the Garden of Eden . . ."

Don Manuel had a knack for saying a lot with his silence.

"We haven't done a very good job of stewardship," I admitted. "And now we're paying quite a price."

"Sounds like your people's God is most powerful," Don Manuel said.

"Yes. Omnipotent. He can do anything."

"Yet your Devil gets away with doing terrible deeds, doesn't he?"

I remembered back to the nuns in Sunday school and my fear of questioning what they were teaching us. Sometimes I would hear a vague answer about the glorious mystery, but other times inquiries were met with corporal punishment, so I learned to keep my mouth shut.

I tried to explain to Don Manuel about sin and our relationship to an all-powerful deity looking down from heaven as best I could remember. "We're taught to pray for God's help. For rescue."

"I see. So the God of your people is either not all-powerful or simply not just or fair. Because he allows people to suffer so."

The face of one particularly authoritarian nun flashed in my mind . . .

"What about your God?" I asked. "Where is he?"

"Where is *she*," he said. He pointed to the fields ready for the harvest, golden stalks of wheat and corn reflecting the bright sunlight at a 12,000-foot altitude. I stood for a moment, catching my breath, taking in the beauty surrounding me.

"Here she is," he said, sweeping his hand from one corner of the horizon to the other, from the mountains to the intense blue sky dotted only by a few billowy clouds and a condor in the distance, wings outstretched.

"We call her Pachamama, the divine mother. She is how Spirit manifests here, and her name means 'the Earth.'" He turned to me, his eyes piercing mine.

"Paradise," I said, awed by the view. "Paradise lost."

He looked at me quizzically.

"According to the Bible, after six days of creating the heavens and the Earth and its inhabitants, including humans and a paradise on Earth, came the seventh day, on which God rested."

"And then?"

I had no answer.

"We do not believe paradise became lost. We believe Mother Earth wants us to complete the work of creation.

Your story—on the seventh day, she didn't rest. She said, 'I have crafted the butterflies and the whales and the eagles. Do you see? Aren't they beautiful? Now you finish it.'"

I thought about how much of the land far below us had been destroyed by developers, how the rivers and skies had become polluted, about how the jungles by the Amazon miles away were disappearing at an alarming rate while at the same time communities are increasingly being devastated by weather events that used to be extremely rare. Here we humans were supposed to be stewards of the Earth, yet we have become so caught up in our earthly activities and need to prove our will that we have fallen asleep on the job. Co-creators with Pachamama—are we really qualified for that position?

"Co-creating," Don Manuel said. "Shall we get on with it?"

Only with the wisdom of the divine feminine can we start finding new ways of being and of relating to our planet and each other. Reclaiming a harmonious relationship with ourselves and the Earth, the work of the North, is more important than ever. It requires letting go of old ideas and behaviors.

Accepting the Reality of Change

Sometimes a change in the state of our health, such as a terrifying diagnosis, completely discombobulates us. Sometimes change comes in the form of a marriage breaking up, an event that deeply unsettles us. And sometimes it appears suddenly one day when we wake up in the morning and are not sure what we believe in anymore. That's why it is so important to transform the four fates into destiny, shifting the architecture of our energy field so that it stops projecting and choreographing its relative reality in the world.

The pace of change in our lifetimes has been disorienting. No wonder we want to stick with the same habits, the same mind-set, the same way of perceiving. It all fits like an old, comfortable pair of slippers. But it does us—and humanity at large—no good to remain stagnant.

To evolve, we will have to give up the stultifying stories that have become unpleasant yet offer the comfort of familiarity. As the saying goes, the devil that you know is preferable to the one you don't. When you're unclear about what move to make next, you will likely talk yourself into what's worked before—even when you strongly sense you're making a mistake. Most people would be happy to sacrifice the old ways if they could be reassured that sacrificing them would not cause any trouble in their everyday lives. (Spoiler alert: It probably will.) However, we also have to let go of what we value—what gives us pride and a sense of belonging, what gives us comfort because it's familiar to us. We have to release all of that and trust that something equally if not more satisfying will take its place.

We have some artifacts, pottery shards, and legends that can help us imagine what the sacred feminine looked like in everyday life long ago. But even without historical records to guide us, we can look to timeless wisdom teachings and open ourselves to a new dream, letting it arise from the dark and mysterious waters of the void as we navigate her currents. And the teachings we seek can be accessed if we are willing to work with her sacred technology: the wisdom wheel.

The Wisdom Wheel of Pachamama

In the traditions of Andean shamans, Mother Earth, or Pachamama, hastens our evolution by helping us shed the past that confines us and let go of our fears—of physical death but also the death of our preconceived notions about who we are and who we can become. Pachamama helps us become wise and see our lives as part of a larger mythic story as we transcend the limitations of all myths, beliefs, and ideas about what is possible. Then we can begin experiencing our inseparable oneness with all of creation. Pachamama offers us healing and wisdom through her wisdom wheel.

We must learn to collaborate with Pachamama and practice ayni—living according to the principle of reciprocity and actively choosing to bring balance and healing to any situation. As I wrote in my book *Island of the Sun*, "You make ayni to the Pachamama, the Mother Earth, and she is pleased and returns your gift with fertility and abundance. You make ayni to the Sun, and he returns your gift with warmth and light. The apus, the great mountain peaks, give you strength to endure your work; the heavens give you harmony. Make ayni to all people and they will honor you in return. It is a beautiful principle. They say that the shaman lives in perfect ayni: the universe reciprocates her every action and mirrors her intent back to her as she is a mirror to others."[2]

We honor Pachamama not just through ayni and collaboration but by reclaiming the lost feminine and its gifts of creativity, nurturance—and destruction. (After all, you can't grow something new if your garden is already filled with roses.) Reality is always changing. We can resist, which will cause us suffering, or we can immerse ourselves in the process of evolution and transformation as we recognize that we, as individuals, are not the only ones co-creating with the universe in a collaborative dance. Going with the flow in perfect ayni will bring us and the Earth back into balance.

Evolution requires awakening to that self that remembers it's all connected—us, Earth, nature and her creatures, our hearts and our heads, our energy and all the particles that make up the body we inhabit for now. Evolution requires us to go beyond the brain to take off the blinders that we inherited and have worn, unquestioningly, for too long and open our eyes to a far broader view of who we are and who we can become—and how we can heal.

CHAPTER 4

THE TRANSFORMATIVE POWER OF THE WISDOM WHEEL

One of the gifts of being married to a medicine woman is that she knows how to pitch a tent, even on the rocky side of a mountain. Marcela had ours up in no time. I was grateful, having made it to the monastery utterly beat from all the hiking we had done.

Last night, I dreamed of serpents: the nagas, who are the snakelike protectors of the temples and who live in the deep rivers and gorges. I dreamed of a mother serpent the length of a football field. She lay on the nearly dry riverbed, her scales and skin parched. She had not been fed in a very long time, and she was dying. She needed the prayers of the people, the offerings of milk and honey the old monks would leave for her on the nature altars.

In the dream, I stroked her head, and she became luminous, radiant, as I caressed her. I was not afraid, only feeling her pain and wanting to soothe her. Then she dissolved into the colors of the rainbow.

In the morning, I told Marcela about my dream. "You helped that ancient naga return to the world of spirit and light. You released her!"

Here's what I have in common with Indiana Jones: I hate snakes. I love them in theory; I appreciate the beauty of the serpent metaphor representing the South, the first direction of the medicine wheel. But when trekking through the jungle and underbrush, I do what I can to avoid snakes. I understood what Marcela meant about helping the naga. I had acquired a certain understanding of the serpent energies, the primordial life force, our urge to begin a creation and transformation process by shedding the old like a skin that no longer fits us.

Marcela said that I had helped the spirit-snake die. I told her it was probably a sexual dream—that the snake, the canyon, the river, and everything else in my dream were different aspects of myself.

"You and psychology!" Marcela replied, shaking her head. "It's not all about you. Please!"

The mind likes to make sense of experiences, drawing on the past to figure out what it all means. Dreams can be the vestiges of memories from the day, but they can also be more than that. Sometimes a cigar is not just a cigar. Sometimes dreams take place not just in our minds and in the synapses between our neurons but in the invisible realm.

In the visible world, nagas symbolize many things. In the invisible place, they are as real as the wind that is sweeping across the mountain and pressing against the sides of the tent.

The conquistadors had no idea how powerful the medicine of the people they had conquered truly was. For one thing, they didn't understand our need to commune with the environment, with microbes that would help us digest foods and our immune system be robust and reject pathogens. They also didn't understand how emotional trauma could damage their health. We now know trauma rewires neural networks in the brain, ensuring that in the present, we continue to be informed by the past—and that can be a problem.

We also know that the effects of trauma can be passed down through the generations via our DNA and that DNA may well carry memories of trauma that the conscious mind knows nothing about. A 2013 study at Emory University found that when mice received shocks accompanied by a release of the scent of cherry blossoms, they passed down a fear of this scent to their offspring and even their grandchildren.[1] Researcher Rachel Yehuda, Ph.D., and her team at the Icahn School of Medicine at Mount Sinai found that an epigenetic marker of a gene related to depression and PTSD was more common in children of Holocaust survivors than in a control group of Jewish people whose parents lived outside of Europe during that time.[2] Additionally, we know that we can affect the expression of our DNA, altering the collection of traumatic memories we will pass to the next generations.

In the modern world, we have few treatments for healing trauma, but the ancients knew that antidotes and healing were available through what they called the medicine wheel, an Indigenous spiritual technology for healing with Mother Earth and the energies of nature and the cosmos.

From Fear to Freedom and Courage

Many initially come to the work of the medicine wheel hoping to heal from physical and emotional ailments. They might not realize there are other gifts of the wheel too: opportunities for reconnection with Spirit, access to the wisdom of sages past and future, and mastery over the fears that hold them back from experiencing greater freedom and well-being.

The medicine or wisdom wheel helps you discover that fear is part of life—it's unavoidable. Learn to master your fear and you may still face some terrifying circumstances right up until you're on your deathbed. However, your life won't be ruled by fear. Fear will serve you as a warning system, as it's meant to, but it will never have you in its grip for very long.

Fear is a primitive response to a real or perceived threat. The body responds instantly to danger so that we can flee to safety, put up a fierce fight, or freeze in the hope that a predator will think we're dead and leave us be. The problem is that in the face of an imagined danger, our brains begin operating like a software program that starts up automatically and sucks up our computer's processing capabilities, completely distracting us from what we want to achieve. To live consciously, free from the perceived fears that weigh us down, including old baggage about how we are supposed to respond and act that has been handed down through the generations, we need a software upgrade. It helps if we also get a hardware upgrade to run the new programming by making dietary and lifestyle changes—you can learn more about the value of those changes in my book *Grow a New Body.*

You will also do the work of the wisdom wheel. In your journey through the wheel, you can release your fear of sickness and dying young and choose a lifestyle and spiritual practice that will lead to a long and healthy life. You can also surrender to the unknown possibilities that you are currently oblivious to because you're afraid of transformation—afraid to change your job, your living situation, your relationship, your image of yourself, and so on.

To Go Deeper, Enter the Spiral

The wisdom wheel is not a two-dimensional circle but a multidimensional spiral that challenges us to go deeper into intense soul-searching work. But before we can change ourselves, our communities, and the planet, creating and bringing to life a new dream, we have a lot to shed. The transformational, evolutionary process of becoming *homo luminous* isn't always going to be pretty.

Consider the caterpillar in the chrysalis. It's cramped in there in the dark, unsure of what's happening, feeling tense and frightened. It doesn't know what it's becoming. It only knows it is losing its caterpillarness, which is all it has ever known. Is it dying? Is it going to disappear? Will it become monstrous and hideous? Will it be miserable in this new form? No matter how uncomfortable the process of change might turn out to be, we can't avoid transformation. We'll end up in that chrysalis, we will feel our fear, but we can learn to move through it and embrace our butterflyness, whatever that looks like. The process takes faith. Recognize that you're not alone, that Spirit is involved in this evolutionary transformation, and you'll find it easier to surrender to what must be and to not knowing the details of what butterflyness will entail.

Then again, not all caterpillars turn into butterflies with colorful wings destined to sip the honey from flowers during the daytime. Close to 90 percent will become moths with dull, colorless wings, flying only at night and eating your wool sweaters.

The only way to ensure that you emerge from a chrysalis into a butterfly with a new way of being and perceiving is to shed your old stories—burn them away in the fire. The task of discarding the worn stories about who you are and what you can expect from life is revitalizing, but be forewarned: it can retrigger all sorts of old wounds and make you feel very discombobulated. Stopping the medicine wheel work at the point where your life force, your Kundalini energy, has been activated if you are still holding on to fear, hurt, resentments, and anger can leave you in a kind of spiritual self-absorption where all you care about is bringing peace and contentment back to your personal life. And you will become a moth.

I have heard many stories of people who sought healing and renewal by traveling to the Amazon and drinking the brew made from the ayahuasca vine. I understand the desire for one quick cure for all our ills, but healing can take time and effort beyond what you anticipate. It can also yield more rewards than you've imagined. In Western culture, the myth of "one big quick fix" is compelling. Who doesn't want a "they lived happily ever after" ending? Stopping your work with the wisdom wheel prematurely can leave you stuck in the chrysalis feeling scared, unsure of what to do, and not knowing who you are or who you are meant to be. Only if you continue to do the work can you access the gifts of the four directions and the four animals that correspond to them.

You will undergo tests of serpent and jaguar that offer you freedom from a fate determined by your genes and your stories about love and what you must do to earn it. The next test will be that of the North and hummingbird. The task here is to shed your notions about why you are here and discover a new sacred path: the way of the sage. You will align with a new map of reality that transforms your personal struggle into an archetypal journey of knowledge, a story that has been told since the dawn of humanity. You will have to be willing to free yourself of the everyday distractions of your mind and your habit of trying to figure everything out based on what you know and your past experiences. You will have to be open to what Zen Buddhists call the beginner's mind—seeing things simply as they are without layering on your personal history, thoughts, or opinions. And you will open to a sense of meaning and purpose that comes from living in ayni with nature and your ancestors.

Your shift into the sacred will let you experience stillness among all the frenetic activity of life and acquire the wisdom of a sage who can draw on the knowledge of the past and the wisdom of the future that you do not yet know. You will start recognizing complexity, nuance, and the synchronistic magical nature of our human experience. We live in a vast sea of impermanence. We can work with that or resist it at great cost to ourselves and the planet and all her creatures. With newfound peace and sage wisdom, the gift of hummingbird, you can start envisioning who you might become and what you might want to experience. Your desire won't be "I want to own a beach house someday" but "I want to feel my connection with the beach, experience the ebb and flow of the tide, and participate in the evolutionary process in a way that feels enriching and enlivening."

Everything on the wisdom wheel journey explodes into brilliant color when you access eagle wisdom: You experience a spiritual awakening that transcends the dogma of the religion in which you were raised. You learn to master time and practice invisibility. And you purify yourself through fire, burning away what's no longer needed and creating an eternal flame of passionate commitment to all that is good. You ask the spirit of the eagle for the gifts of vision and flight: of perceiving the nature of the quantum field, of seeing into the past and into the future, of peering deep into people's souls—and of infusing the sacred into the everyday. The greatest gift is that of envisioning what is possible for our human race. Each small light, in unison with others, has the potential for profound transformation and for the manifestation of a new human.

Who are you to do this envisioning? You are one of all the many people who are dreaming the world into being. Dream well so that we can all break out of this nightmare of perpetual conflict and competition. There is a better way to live together on Earth. The work of the wisdom wheel isn't simply personal. Shamans say you focus first on what the world needs, then on what your community needs, and only then on what you need. One of my teachers said, "Do the math. Twenty percent of your focus can be on yourself and twenty on your community, but sixty percent should be on healing the cosmos." With this focus, your perceptions shift naturally as you gain knowledge and change the way you operate in the everyday world. You see the big picture and don't get caught up in the dramas of your life. You're able to handle the big shifts that happen outside of your control.

Gateways to the Lower and Upper Worlds

When you work with the wisdom wheel, you will encounter gateways into the invisible realms: the lower world and the upper world. Remember what I said: the wheel looks like a circle but is multidimensional. Go deeper into the spiral that takes you downward, and you will reach the world of the past and the ancestors. You can travel below the surface of your awareness in the middle world of everyday experiences. Descent into the lower world takes you into the realm of roots, of secrets of the past and the forgotten history of humanity, including the memories of old wounds. Here in this mystical realm, you can heal from your genetic legacy by making peace with the ancestors and repairing what people in the East would call karma, the habit that the past has of repeating itself.

If you ascend through the wheel into the upper world in the invisible realm beyond the reach of our ordinary senses, you are in the forest canopy. Here, you encounter spirit guides. They can help you discover a new destiny that will take you beyond the confines of the fate determined for you by your past, which has sent you on your current trajectory. In a sense, the work of the upper world allows you to be reborn into a new you—to start forming who you will become.

The lower and upper worlds are connected to us here in the visible realm of the middle world. There, we walk among the trunks of the great trees, knowing of their roots underground and their branches high up above but not able to see the full extent of the majestic world tree that grows right through the middle of the wisdom wheel, reaching down into the Earth and high up into the heavens.

You can develop the ability to cross through these gateways to the invisible realms by doing the work of the wisdom wheel and experiencing liminal consciousness through the use of rituals and ceremonies.

It's important to remember the multidimensional nature of the wisdom wheel. The more shamanic practice you do, the more you'll be in awe of its complexity and even its power to help you make giant leaps in your evolution.

The medicine people see the universe as actively conspiring on our behalf if we let ourselves be guided by a vision co-created with Spirit. The universe collaborates with us in many ways. When we align with it, we are in ayni—in harmony with its loving and wise ways, giving and receiving in balance. Contrast this with a greed-driven way of living in which there's never enough to quell your fear and let you relax into the peacefulness of knowing that the universe supports you. There is never enough money, security, or power to keep the fear at bay. It seems something or someone is always nipping at your heels, ready to pounce and take away all you have. The only real cure for that feeling that life's an endless battle for survival of the fittest is to be in ayni.

The wisdom wheel allows us to use our healing, exploratory, sage, and visionary powers to co-create a much better world for ourselves, for other people, and for Mother Earth herself.

Retrieving a Power Animal to Help You

In addition to the work you'll do in the next chapters with serpent, jaguar, hummingbird, and/or eagle, you can retrieve a power animal that can lend its energy to you. We all have different experiences of these archetypal animal energies. Set your attention to encounter and work with the right power animal to help you with your work, and Pachamama will send the right spirit animal to you. The word *animal* comes from the Latin *anima*, which means "spirit" or "soul." These beings are the spirit of Pachamama, powerful nature guides that will aid you in resetting your instinct and retrieving your undomesticated nature. After finding your power animal, you call on it regularly to guide you in making the right choices and decisions in your life using the conversation technique described in this ceremony. Ask it whatever you like—but know that it might be easier to gain answers if you've quieted your busy brain and mind to better hear what your power animal has to tell you.

Journey to the Island of Sacred Animals

To begin this guided meditation, get into a comfortable position, close your eyes, and focus on your breathing. If your mind wanders, draw your attention back to your breathing again until you feel relaxed and you shift out of your busy mind.

Imagine yourself sitting on a flat rock at the top of a mountain, surrounded by trees on all sides except one, where there is a gentle downslope. As you gaze into the distance, you see that at the base of the mountain is a meadow, and beyond the meadow is a beach and the ocean. Far off, you see a large bank of fog that slowly begins to dissipate and clear. Through the mist, you make out the outlines of an island. You realize that you are looking at the Island of Sacred Animals, and you feel yourself drawn to visit it.

Now that the fog has cleared and the island is visible, you begin to make your way down the mountain, following the gentle slope until you get to the grassy meadow below. You continue walking toward the beach, feeling the warm sand beneath your feet and the cool breeze against your skin. You smell the ocean . . . feel the saltiness in the air. You hear the waves breaking gently on the sand and seabirds calling to each other as they fly overhead.

To your left, you notice that there is a spirit canoe on the shore. You hesitate for a moment . . . then realize that the spirit canoe is here for you to take you to the Island of Sacred Animals. You push the canoe out onto the shallow water and climb into it. And you notice that there is a paddle. You take it and begin to make your way toward the island.

With each stroke, strength surges through your body. You find yourself paddling as if through a dream. . . A light mist surrounds you as the island draws closer. The water sparkles as you glide effortlessly to the island. And now you feel the bow of the boat scraping against the sandy shore. You jump out of the canoe and pull it ashore.

You look around you. The ocean waves are lapping gently against the shore. The fine sand is like a carpet bounded on one side by the sea and on the other by a forest of tall trees. There is a stream that leads deep into the woods, and you sense that far within it is a lake. And out of the corner of your eye, you begin to sense animals nearby. You feel they are looking at you. You catch a glimpse of what seems to be a lion, and then a lynx . . . perhaps a unicorn . . . and an eagle . . . and a deer. They are all here, and you feel an invitation to explore the island.

You might find yourself walking along the sea or into the forest or the brush . . . or along the river. Follow to where your heart takes you until you find a clearing. In the center of the clearing is an animal that you sense wants to meet you. It might be standing in the middle of the clearing or by a tree as you pass by. Or it may be flying above or swimming near you. You will recognize it as your power animal because it will gaze right into your eyes . . . and it will touch you in some way.

As you come close to your power animal, greet it with respect and look into its eyes. Ask your power animal to share the lessons it has for you. What is it saying to you? Ask it anything you like. What kind of power or wisdom does it have for you? What can you do for it so that you and this animal can have a reciprocal relationship?

And now you look up in the sky and realize that it's getting dark, that it's time to leave the island. You invite your power animal to return with you back to the familiar shores of your world. And you begin to make your way back to the beach, back to your spirit canoe. Before you step in, you turn and see other sacred animals watching you from behind trees. All of them are taking their leave from you, saying good-bye in their own way. You thank them as you board your spirit canoe. As you begin to paddle and make your way back, you look beside you and realize that your power animal is sitting next to you, returning with you— or perhaps you are bringing back only the memory of your meeting with the power animal. It's okay either way.

Continue making your way back, feeling your paddle cutting through the waves. The sea is becoming a bit choppy, and the sky is becoming darker. The return journey seems longer; it takes greater effort. But you have the force and energy of your power animal with you, and with each stroke of your paddle, you feel your energy and power surging.

Finally, the shore draws near. You beach your spirit canoe and step out. And you turn and see that again, the island is enveloped in fog, enshrouded in mist. You walk upon the beach and into the meadow where you sit down, close your eyes, and invite your power animal to remain with you. This is your ally. Realize that the force, the strength, and the knowledge of this animal is yours.

You reach out with one hand, keeping your eyes closed, and you feel your power animal next to you. You feel its fur or its wings or its scales . . . its belly, its face . . . you know that it is a manifestation of the divine in the natural world.

Now take five deep breaths and bring yourself back to the ordinary world, to your room and to your body. Open your eyes and gently, slowly, sit up.

Visit with your power animal toward the end of each of the fire ceremonies you'll find in this book. And invite it into your dreams right before you fall asleep. In doing this, you're inviting an aspect of Mother Earth to help you.

Dialogue with your power animal using the following exercise: Draw a line down the middle of a sheet of paper. Place your name on the top left and your power animal on the top right side of the page. Begin by asking your power animal, "Who are you? Why did you come to me? What are your gifts?" What lessons must I learn?" Consult with your power animal as you do the work of each of the directions to find its guidance and follow its natural instincts, which are now yours.

Part II

TRANSFORMATION

CHAPTER 5

SERPENT WISDOM
(THE SOUTH)

After one day, Amchi Tenjing Bista arrived at last with the horses after a six-day journey from Lo Manthang, leading a pack of Mustangs full gallop over the mountains. Joan had told me that he was happiest when he was on a horse or when taking the pulses of a patient. An interesting combination—doctor and cowboy.

We were shown which of the horses he had brought were for riding and which were for carrying our luggage and medical supplies. Amchi had brought his own medicine with him, plants and herbs and pills that he used to treat one of the four categories of disease in Tibetan medicine, which are caused by ailments and trauma from this and earlier lives.

Amchi explained to me that the Tibetans recognize 404 different diseases:

- *101 untreatable karmic diseases that are caused by your actions in the present and previous lifetimes*

- *101 diseases caused by evil spirits, negative forces, jealousy, envy, and anger*

- *101 diseases in this lifetime that stem from childhood events*

- *101 lifestyle diseases that you can correct by changing your diet and behavior without having to resort to medication*

These were pretty much the same categories of ailments that shamans in the Americas that I had worked with recognized. I knew that Amchi and I would have much to talk about.

Every third day of our trek, we would stop to set up the Nomad Clinic, and word would go out that doctors had arrived. Soon we would see people coming—almost always on foot, sometimes carrying a sick person on their back. I wondered how many miles they had logged getting to us. By early morning, dozens of villagers would be lined up waiting to be examined by the physicians in our team. Our Western doctors could do little more than diagnose. Our medical supplies were very limited, and with no blood labs, no MRI or ultrasound or X-ray machines, the doctors simply had to do their best to identify what was causing the pain or discomfort and what could be done about it. These very wonderful men and women were very much at a loss. The best they were able to do in most cases was give some lifestyle advice, suggest that the patient travel to the hospital a week's walk away, or hand them a pair of reading glasses and a toothbrush, or perhaps aspirin or ibuprofen.

Amchi was different. During his examinations, he would take the patient's hand and feel their pulse. While this was his main diagnostic technique, I could see he was taking in more than simply how quick and strong each person's heartbeat was. And I could see he was not treating the disease but the person. He gave everyone medicine, sometimes for the condition they suffered from, other times an herbal tea for their life of hardship. I wanted to learn about that medicine. Who couldn't use a little help with the burdens of everyday life?

I asked him what was in the teapot.

"Chamomile tea," he said.

My face must have betrayed my confusion.

"It's how you prepare it," Amchi explained. "With love."

The journey through the wisdom wheel begins in the South, where you learn to shed your past like a serpent sheds her skin. By doing this, you can become unencumbered by family drama, no longer fated to develop the physical ailments that your family of origin suffered or repeat old psychological patterns related to them. But shedding the past is not easy. The tragic stories and ailments do not go away by magic. They have to be burned and consumed by an inner fire generated by awakening the power of the coiled serpent: the Kundalini power.

You must acquire serpent wisdom if you want to use this inner fire for warmth rather than for burning the house down. That doesn't mean disowning your past; it means no longer being owned by it. It means shedding your excuses for why your life isn't working as you would like it to. When you truly shed your past and all its stories, you are no longer the product of only your upbringing or your tragic family tales or stories of fortunes lost and love betrayed. With serpent wisdom, the deepest healing of the old wounds, including the wounds of your family and people, begins.

If you aren't determined to shed all the past, you will end up only half out of the old skin, holding on to the stories that bring you comfort and preventing yourself from experiencing something even better. You will unwittingly re-create those old stories. In the South, you can't shed a few things that you think you ought to get rid of bit by bit so as to reduce any discomfort, keeping them close at hand just in case you need them. You are not going to have a "junk drawer" full of all the tales you might want to tell someday. No, you're going to bet all your chips on the next roll of the dice. You are going to shed your whole past and all of its stories, knowing that it is your determination and intention that set the level of the play and allow you to engage forces bigger than you are.

If you succeed, you might experience a moment of blissful nonbeing as you lose all sense of your wounded self for a brief time. In that moment, you will no longer be defined by the drama and disease that runs in your family. You can step out of that stale fate and into a higher destiny.

The serpent knows the ways to the depths of your psyche and the hidden places in your soul where you must heal your deepest wounds and find your greatest treasures. She knows how to lead you to the innermost sacred feminine, which she represents, and the stories you would rather forget that became hidden beneath the ones you told yourself to feel in control of your personal narrative. She leads you into a deep dive into the mysterious, dark depths of the Great Mother Earth, where you are stripped of everything that is not of your authentic self. If you are fortunate, she will swallow you whole. Her bottomless love and terrifying presence will set your life on fire to begin to clear the way for you to experience your interconnection with all that exists. She will remind you of who you really are beyond your limited ideas about your identity, which have been shaped by your family legacy.

With the help of serpent, you can see that yours was neither a happy nor an unhappy childhood. The gift is the ability to accept that what happened was what happened and not attach any stories, positive or negative, to your memoires. Attain the serpent's gift and you will feel much less compelled to tell people your personal tale of what you have suffered and overcome. You'll find you're less interested in what was than in "What now?" and "What might be?" and "Who might I become?" You will not forget what happened as a result of doing the work of the serpent, but your memories will live differently within you, no longer restricting you to live according to the fate that was preselected for you when you were born into your family and began adopting its patterns.

The deepest work of the South requires that we encounter the mythic serpent, known as a naga, and its fierceness.

According to legends of India and Tibet, a naga is a great sea serpent from the depths of the river or the oceans and a keeper of treasures and wisdom. In Hindu lore, nagas are deities that can assume any form they wish, particularly human and serpent forms. They dwell in an enchanted underworld, serving as guardians of precious treasures. Their preferred abodes are the lakes, rivers, and oceans, and they are believed to have such power and venom that they are particularly dangerous to humans. The nagas urge you to let go of who you thought you were and what limitations you have so that you can find hidden treasures—strengths, opportunities, ideas, and wisdom. Nagas are not pleased when you hold on to the past and your fear of the unknown. Will we meet the naga's challenge? Will we muster the courage that Eve had to accept the fruit of the tree of knowledge, despite suspecting the consequences?

The naga is internalized as the Kundalini, the life force of Mother Earth that awakens in your lower chakras and rises through your energy centers. Once you awaken this energy, don't abandon it. Keep working with it. Use it for transformation and reinvention. Change is nature's way. Make it your way, because change is going to happen anyway.

Don't Resist the New Skin

Admittedly, getting used to a new and unfamiliar skin is uncomfortable at first. Even so, keep working on shedding the old ways and the old tales, including the ones of physical and emotional ills that you inherited.

You have to remain vigilant, however, because when serpent energy is first awakened, you can become determined to right old wrongs and to start defining your life by the rejection of your family legacy, which is not that much of a leap from continuing your family legacy. The idea is to be freed from the grip of your unconscious legacy and its physical ailments and ills so you can be blessed by it when appropriate but not driven to repeat it or reject it.

Keep in mind that you were developing ideas about reality from the moment you were conceived, and your perceptions continued to form with every experience you had. Stories that your family and the people you knew as a child passed down to you may have been composed long before your great-great-great-grandparents were born. Your parents might not even have been aware of the narratives they were handing over to you. Stories of magical rescuers swooping in, stories of following all the rules and working hard to be assured a good, happy, long, and healthy life—these are tales that you probably heard told in many ways and didn't look at closely or question. I remember as a boy hearing that all the men in our family lost their hair by their midtwenties and became determined not to lose my hair, or for that matter, my mind, like the elderly men in my family had.

If you believed those stories and suddenly realized that they have not come true, then you might question other beliefs that have shaped your life and perceptions. Even so, you might find yourself unable to stop believing in them anyway, feeling a duty to your parents.

The myth of being cast out of paradise dwells in the Western psyche whether or not people were raised in an Abrahamic religion. All of us have myths we absorbed along the way, ways of perceiving that we adopted unwittingly back in childhood, which are woven into our brains. What your parents, grandparents, aunts, and uncles told you back in your early years most likely stuck in your psyche much more firmly than you realize. The work of the South is to identify these exhausted myths and let go of them into the fire. You are likely to find that as a result, you write your personal story differently.

Maybe you will be a teacher just like your parents were but teach in a new way. You might become a parent but parent differently from how your parents and their parents before them did it. You might change the ways in which you express your femininity or masculinity, how you act as a "good person" or "loyal son" or "loving daughter." Many possibilities are hidden from sight while you are afraid to let go of the past and your family stories.

These psychological stories also seem to be physiological. Researcher Rachel Yehuda of the Icahn School of Medicine at Mount Sinai discovered that children of Holocaust survivors had epigenetic markers for differences in levels of the stress hormone cortisol. Economist Dora Costa of UCLA studied U.S. Civil War POW records, noting what happened to their sons who were born after they went to war, were captured, and experienced starvation in prison camps. These sons had an 11 percent higher rate of mortality (mostly from cerebral hemorrhage and cancer) than sons of veterans who weren't taken prisoner. Looking at the records of POWs' sons who were born before the war, she found that there was no increased mortality rate. (This phenomenon was only observed in sons, not daughters.)

It's not easy to tease out whether traumatized parents' behavior with their children is the source of differences in epigenetics. However, researcher Isabelle Mansuy of the University of Zürich and ETH Zürich has studied intergenerational trauma in mice for up to six generations and found that the effects on offspring raised away from their traumatized fathers continued to be seen. Of course, these studies are only preliminary, and because lifestyle choices can change epigenetics, biology isn't destiny. What's important to remember is that the physiological inheritance of trauma and old stories might be far greater than science has revealed so far.[1]

Stories of exploration and discovery, of caring for others and loving yourself, can create health. Stories of anger, failure, and resentment can create sickness and disease. You only need to look at the illnesses that run in your family that are part of your genetic legacy and see them as metaphors to trace them back to the myth that gave rise to them. Think about when heartbreak turned into heart disease, hardening of the soul became stiffness in the arteries and arteriosclerosis, suppressed anger turned into liver disease, and fear became a cancer. Personal myths will continue to survive in the pool of memory your family of origin shares, but shedding those stories will free you to choose healthy ones about who you are becoming. Remember that for the shamans, illnesses do not exist—only sick people. Illnesses are a symptom and expression of the story you are living and the myths that possess you.

By shedding your past like the serpent sheds her skin, you free yourself to create something new—a destiny not determined by your family legacy. But first, you must experience the unsettling feeling of being present in a void.

Nagas and the Void

Nāgārjuna, an Indian sage and philosopher who flourished in the 2nd century B.C.E. and whose name means "the one who tames the nagas," is credited with articulating the deepest of Buddhist teachings on sunyata, or the nature of emptiness. He challenged the basic assumptions that most of us hold about the world and reality. Nāgārjuna asserted that all beings, and all phenomena, are devoid of selfness. This does not mean that the table in front of you does not exist; it means that the table has no unique "tableness." I have no unique "Albertoness." All phenomena, including you and I, are devoid of independent existence. We are deeply interconnected with each other much like the roots of the trees in the forest. Thus, everything that I believe myself to be (human, man, author, shaman, father), my qualities that I highly treasure and identify with, emanates from the quantum field, to use the language of physics. We emerge from the energy field that permeates the cosmos, and eventually, we return to it. And while it seems we are separated from it, and that we each have a unique and independent existence and reality, that's an illusion. We are never truly separate from the field. Emptiness is the true nature of reality. But don't get depressed about that, because as it turns out, emptiness is not empty—at least, not in the way we think.

I know it sounds like a riddle, and I have found that there is nothing as frustrating as hearing a Tibetan monk speak for three hours on the nature of emptiness. After fifteen minutes, I am squirming in my chair and saying to myself, *If everything is empty of essence, why are you going on so much about it?*

For the shaman, the emptiness holds limitless potential for you to create something original and authentic. And what arises out of this void is a story buzzing with possibility, one that can create health and order—or disease and disorder and pain. This is why so many of the ancient gods of the Americas are depicted with a song coming from their mouths, and why even in Western culture, we believe that in the beginning there was the word, a story.

Some shamans have the experience of emptiness during ceremonies with the medicine plants. I have found myself many times during an ayahuasca ceremony in the Amazon on the banks of the Mother of God River feeling at one with the rain forest, with all its creatures, and with the stars above. I remember one night when I was basking in the bliss of this oneness, I wondered where I was. I realized that I had ceased to exist as a separate being. I could not find myself, only the vastness of space. And I was in complete bliss, experiencing gnosis, because in that emptiness lies limitless possibilities and infinite wisdom.

And then someone coughed, and boom, that sense of oneness disappeared.

The good news is that I didn't forget what happened. Too many people do. It seems like a dream, that taste of infinity. However, just that brief taste has also led people to completely transform their lives and write a better story for themselves.

The shaman realizes her serpent power and wisdom when she discovers the nature of the void, the blank spot on the map of her journey. It is when we have emptied ourselves of all our stories and roles and allowed ourselves to feel completely lost in the middle of nowhere, lacking maps and a compass, that something extraordinary happens. That's when we become the storyteller and not the story, the dreamer and not the dream.

The experience of emptiness, gnosis, and the awakening that happens—as if your eyes were open for the first time—can't be taught with words. Language can only hint at the experience that became the basis of all Tibetan Buddhism. Only when you fully realize these lessons will you be able to understand the dreamlike nature of reality and how to "dream the world into being."

You've got a lot of work and learning to do on the way there. The deep healing that you will do if you meet the challenge of the South is a healing of the story before it coalesced into form.

The Nagas' Challenge to You

So how do you experience the liberation and freedom from all that you believe to be real and true in order to become open to a vast array of possibilities? How do you shed your limitations, including those created by people long gone who determined what your life on this planet should look like? You can start by using practices known to shift consciousness.

One of those is meditation, which can take you to an experience of the Mother of the Buddhas, known as the Prajnaparamita to Tibetans, the place of infinite wisdom-bliss. This is the perfected way of seeing the nature of reality, unobscured by appearances, and understanding that everything from the grossest of objects to the most luminous Buddha is devoid of independent existence. We are all related. The Lakota people of North America look out into nature and say, "Mitákuye Oyás'iŋ, all my relations," greeting the buzzing insects, the rushing river, and the birds in the sky as if they were their brothers or sisters or cousins— because they are. Spend some time in nature simply being among the feathered and the scaled, remembering your true relationship with them ought to be one of ayni, reciprocity, which you will learn more about in Chapter 7: Hummingbird Wisdom (The North).

Another practice that will lead you to discover the nature of infinite wisdom-bliss is the fire ceremony, and that's one we will focus on in this book, as it is the most ancient of all the shamanic practices. I do not consider myself a good meditator, yet I love sitting around the embers of a fire, allowing the volume in my mind to drop as I sit in the presence of red-hot coals and flickering flames. When you place a log into the fire, contemplate how the form disappears into light as the essence of the wood is released. And think of how someday your light will also be released and you will return to the great all, devoid of name and form. Fire ceremonies activate our intuitive understanding of the transformative power of the Kundalini, the primordial serpent energy, as well as our ancestral memories of gathering around the fire with others for warmth, nourishment, and companionship. You can do the fire ceremonies alone or with others; I'll leave that up to you.

And you'll want to do these ceremonies often, even daily. In my early days in the Amazon as a young medical anthropologist, experiences where my separateness or Albertoness dissolved and overwhelming bliss took its place were fleeting. I would look forward to each ceremony, where I would flood my brain with sacred jungle medicine to experience oneness with all. Later, I realized that I lacked the discipline and the steadfastness that you develop through meditation or prayer (or shamanic journeying to the invisible world). My extraordinary experiences would begin to fade by the following morning, and a couple days later, they would be gone, having left behind faint memories of an amazing "trip." How do you get to oneness more often to experience your authentic self regularly? The same way you get to Carnegie Hall, as the old joke goes: practice, practice, practice.

RT (Rolling Thunder) was quite adept at entering into a higher state of consciousness that shamans say allows you to interact with the quantum field. One night a few years ago, I was suffering with hepatitis and was very ill, and I took a bath in my tub at home to try to release the toxins and stress that were wiping me out each day. A candle I'd placed on the sink was flickering, casting shadows, when suddenly, on the edge of the tub, at my feet, there emerged an eagle who seemed intent on picking something from her talons with her beak. I was stricken with fear, but the eagle perched gently on my feet and started to soothe me with its wings.

"I am here," he said, speaking directly to my consciousness, "to turn your sickness into healing and to teach you to fly." Suddenly, I realized this was not just any spirit eagle; he was my friend RT. The next time I saw him, I said, "You scared me when you came to me as the eagle." RT gave me a knowing smile in response.

A shaman must journey to the depths of her own psyche and beyond to meet the powerful nagas and be offered their wisdom gift—in the same way that Nāgārjuna traveled to the bottom of the sea and into the fabric of time itself to retrieve the teachings on emptiness. The goal is to experience their power and take them into your consciousness rather than simply understanding the serpent power intellectually. But let's start with the teachings.

There are two levels of truth, both equally valid depending on the observer's point of reference in the same way that Newtonian physics (the understanding of how large objects work) and quantum mechanics (how exquisitely small units of matter or light work) are both valid. The first level of truth is relative truth, which attributes reality and self-existence to objects and to people: you are someone and hope to grow up to become more truly yourself. The second level is absolute truth: everything is empty of selfness. This is not a cause for despair but a vehicle to achieve liberation.

Everything that you believe that you are and everything that you own also owns you. Some people give away everything they own. Jesus encouraged people he met to do this and follow him. But the letting go of the old identity and the trappings of it must be at a deeper level than giving away your old business suits or your dreams of being important or even of being happy. Your letting go is temporary, like taking off a pair of sunglasses so that you can experience unfiltered light. If you're not willing to shed your identity to experience the terror of the void and its limitless potential, you're likely to overlook new possibilities that could lead to a profound and desirable transformation.

In Western culture, we are likely to have been told that if we do not know who we are, it is a problem that must be solved. We are often told that we ought to go to a therapist to help us find out. A psychologist can then help us discover who we are and who we want to be instead—or help us improve upon who we are in some way. In Tibet, it's the complete opposite. When you discover you have no idea who you are, it's time for a celebration. Congratulations! You are in an exalted state! You wake up in the morning and look at yourself in the mirror and say, "I don't know who you are, but I will prepare breakfast for you anyway!" Much discovery awaits you.

This notion of nonbeing, ridding yourself of all the ideas about the self and remaining present in a state of nonknowing and nondoing, can be hard to grasp. We live in a world where people often find themselves more focused on how to present the best curated version of themselves, and on how people see them, than on simply staying present in the moment, waiting to see what emerges in the space between breaths.

If you do enter into this state of liberation in which you feel a deep sense of unity with the void, even if only for just a few exhilarating seconds, it's best not to spend more time thinking and talking about it than you do preparing to experience it again. Spending time in a state beyond selfness and selfishness in the void of potential that turns out not to be empty but filled with possibility starts to rewire your brain and get rid of old programming. Then you don't find yourself automatically falling back into old ways when triggered by a situation that seems familiar. Instead, you say, "Wow, what is this? What's happening? Let me check it out!" Your conflict with your usual nemesis is completely different because you have changed. You don't feel that adrenaline rush that you used to feel. You start looking at this other person with new eyes, the eyes of a new individual (you) who is wearing your clothes. This new you can observe your fear, as well as that of others, where once you would have only seen each other's anger and aggression. At this point, your new skin doesn't feel quite so odd like it did before. You recognize it as yours. And it feels good.

Encountering the Energy

The nagas you encounter in the depths of your being are the personified powers of nature that offer the gift of potentiality that lies within the void. But they will not surrender this if you come to them empty-handed and not do any work. Sheath your sword; there's no need to battle them. Instead, bring them an offering of milk. The nagas know you don't exist as a name, or "the son or daughter of . . . ," or a collection of experiences and life drama, but you do not want to be confused for a naga's lunch. The milk you bring is the milk of kindness and love. Even so, in all likelihood, the naga will open its mouth and show you its fangs to test if you have truly let go of everything, including your fear and your belief that maybe you can change just a little bit, no more than is absolutely necessary. Nagas do not appreciate your coming to them asking for great power only to use it to fix a few minor problems.

You need to dive deeper and be courageous.

It can be exhilarating to shed old skin if it hasn't been serving you well. It can be even more exhilarating to step into that void of not knowing who you are now if you're not who you thought you were and always will be. However, both can be terrifying. Who are you if you aren't all those things you thought mattered?

Who is this "you"? You are your authentic self that has too often become hidden from sight by all the muck cluttering up your view of yourself in all your beauty. Your wiracocha is obscured, and your light has become dimmed by the detritus and fog of your past suffering and even that of your family and ancestors. Your goal is to let it shine.

If you were raised with one of the Western religions, you have to make an extra effort to find the wisdom and power of the serpent medicine, because snakes have been vilified and demonized. After all, the first experience we have with a naga in the Bible is with the serpent that tempted Eve to eat the fruit of the tree of knowledge and got her— and humanity—expelled from paradise. Christianity has associated the serpent with evil, sexuality, and, destructively, the feminine. Most of us have been taught that the serpent is not to be trusted. It is said to use trickery to separate us from God, which is why St. Patrick drove all the snakes from Ireland, or so the legend goes. The story is a metaphor for driving out the old spiritual traditions that predated Christianity, the ones that recognized the power and beauty of the sacred feminine.

When I write about the nagas and what the serpent represents, I'm not speaking of symbols. You might prefer that I stick to strictly psychological language here and stop with all this mythology. But when you begin to follow a path, you enter a mythic bubble: all of the sacred elements of that myth cease being symbols and become accessible to you as a direct experience. You finally get it in your gut and in every fiber of your being, not just intellectually.

This is true whether you are a Christian and start to have dreams and/or visions of the Madonna or of the saints, or if you are a Hindu and sense the presence of Shiva during meditation. This is also true if you consider yourself an atheist or agnostic but find yourself in the presence of what you somehow know to be a guardian angel. And it is true if you receive communication from the spirit of someone who is long dead yet right there in front of you, unseen but as real as the ground you are standing on. The nagas become not just a symbol but a reality—one that is difficult to describe. You might want to share it with others, but you suspect they'll think you're not in your right mind. Because what you have experienced took place in the invisible world of Spirit.

You did not imagine it.

Beyond Words, Beyond Rituals

The House of the Virgin Mary is a Catholic shrine located on Mount Koressos near Ephesus, Turkey. Catholic pilgrims visit this site because they believe that Mary, the mother of Jesus, was brought there by the Apostle John after Christ's crucifixion and lived there for the remainder of her life on Earth. Shortly after the death of my father, my mother, a devout Catholic, planned a trip to Turkey and visited this site. When she entered the small chapel, she said a brief prayer and, feeling a bit claustrophobic, walked outside by the "wishing wall," where pilgrims leave pieces of paper or fabric with their prayers inscribed on them.

My parents were fortunate to have enjoyed a loving marriage for more than 50 years. After my father's passing, my mother entered into a deep depression. She felt vulnerable and alone in the world and wasn't sure she could endure a lonely life for much longer. After leaving her prayer at the wall, she walked to a nearby spring, where she felt someone place a hand on her shoulder. Simultaneously, she heard a clear female voice say to her, "Elena, you will never be alone. I will always be with you. I will never leave your side."

Startled, she looked around, but there was no one near her. And the voice had spoken to her in Spanish, her native tongue.

That afternoon, my mother's mood began to lift. Within a few days, she had recovered her optimism and strength and had a newfound joy. Within the year, she met the man that she would marry and spend the later years of her life with. And every night as she said her prayers, she could sense the presence of the Madonna by her side.

When she told me this story, I had been to the House of the Virgin Mary on a trip to Turkey and found it to be completely unimpressive. The wishing wall reminded me of the hope that all religions offer their followers who seek divine intervention to recover their health or get a nicer house or car. I had no interest in ever visiting the site again. I reminded my mother that archaeologists had established that this site was not occupied before the 12th century and never could have been the abode of Mary.

"Well, she must have moved in recently," my mother said firmly, convinced that the Madonna had touched her and spoken to her.

"True," I said, "that was probably what happened!"

I lost my interest in offering archaeological evidence about the site. My mother's depression had cleared, and she became a happy woman. I figured, who am I to argue with miracles?

Today, I realize that every spiritual tradition has a sacred, special, mythic bubble that envelops it. Once you enter that bubble, you begin to experience its gods, demons, gifts, and temptations, and that tradition's path becomes palpable. You begin to follow a mystical map to God, or Spirit, or heaven.

But you do not even have to join the tradition. All you need to do is to step into one of its sacred bubbles. My wife is part Native American, and even though she had been raised in a very Catholic country, she had been initiated into Buddhism at an early age. As she grew older, she identified with the women shamans of Chile, the machi, and all religion fell to the wayside. Her mother had tried on numerous occasions to get her to church to no avail—that is, until we went to Notre-Dame Cathedral in Paris.

We were simply visiting. I was more interested in the grand stained glass windows, particularly the west rose that dates from the year 1225, than the mass being celebrated in the main altar. I had attended far too many masses in my youth, and although a devout admirer of Christ, I have had little interest in the liturgy. I turned to look for Marcela and saw her in a pew, deep in prayer. When I walked over to her, she announced she was going to go up for her first

Communion. She had never tasted the wafer that in Christianity represents the body of Christ. (Actually, according to Catholic tradition, it does not *represent* the body of Christ. Once it has been blessed, handed to the supplicant by the priest, and placed in the mouth, it *is* the body of Christ.)

When I asked Marcela what had happened, she pointed to the statue of the Madonna to the right of the altar.

"She called me to her," she explained. "I understood that she was the same goddess that we honor. The Pachamama. Mother Earth."

I know better than to argue with a shaman, particularly the one that I am married to, so I followed Marcela down the aisle to the altar, where the priest was offering participants the bread that had been transformed by the greatest miracle in the Catholic Church into the body of the Savior. I said a quick prayer asking to be absolved of all my sins, which were too many to list, and joined Marcela in Communion.

One of the gifts of the way of the shaman, since it is not a religion, is that it allows us to find the joy and beauty in all religions, whether it is Christianity, Hinduism, Buddhism, or something else. Their sacred bubbles are available to us because we do not adhere to exclusionary dogma or belief that any one way is better; we base our knowledge on experience. We may struggle with the teachings of these traditions because of past baggage, but that day Marcela reminded me to shed all that keeps us from experiencing the power of sacred, healing love. We must empty ourselves.

As shamans, we are mapmakers—cartographers of the soul. We may follow another's maps for a while until we discover that the truths embedded in that map, the landscapes of the soul's journey, feel incomplete to us. The map expresses the truths of others, not of ourselves. We realize we don't have to follow the path of our family or our community of friends and like-minded people. We don't have to restrict ourselves to a landscape defined by people whose past experiences of suffering and betrayal shaped their identity. We have agency to alter the map or create an entirely new one.

Once, after Don Manuel and I had eaten a meal together at the home of a friend of his, I mentioned that while I had eaten this traditional soup before many times on my travels through Peru, it had never tasted quite like this. "Every cook finds their own way," Don Manuel said. "Your problem is you are still afraid to change even one ingredient."

I complained that I was an anthropologist, that it was my job to observe, chronicle, and document, not to change the ingredients of the soup. It was not up to me to alter the way shamans perform rituals or the way they talk about their beliefs and the work they do.

"You are a paco," he said, "a shaman of your people. You have a calling and a mission. Anthropologists? They are like buzzards fighting over the carcasses of an ancient people like ours, picking out the strips of flesh they can steal to feast on."

We must be careful not to set our hearts on what we are supposed to experience. If we let go of our expectations, what is supposed to happen can do so.

Shedding in the Sweat Lodge

The first time I visited Rolling Thunder at his ranch, Meta Tantay, he invited me to join a sweat lodge ceremony that evening. I pitched my tent in the backyard and helped the young men and women who were tending the fire to heat the rocks we would be using in the lodge. Later we prepared prayer ties, organic tobacco wrapped into pieces of white cloth that we hung from the willow branches that formed the skeleton of the lodge. We then covered the hut, which looked like an upside-down bowl, with blankets.

At around 10 P.M., as the daylight finally gave way to the dark and the stars came out, RT summoned us and led a prayer to the four directions, calling on the guardians of each of the four corners of the world to protect and guide us. We then touched our foreheads to the Earth as we entered the lodge one by one.

Once we were all inside, RT explained that the heat of the darkened lodge would help melt away our impure ways—that we had become disconnected, fragmented, and strayed from the ways of the Earth and of nature. This was the cause of all ailments. We were like children who denied their mother and refused her bounty while looting and pillaging her forests and oceans. We had to let go of the white man's domineering and destructive ways.

We spent hours in the lodge. I lost count of how many times we exited and reentered it. Each round of stepping out into the night air was called a "door." RT explained that "the person that left the lodge is not the same person that entered." We were going deeper and deeper into a spiral, descending into the Earth, returning to our mother's womb. The idea was to return renewed, reborn.

Halfway into the ceremony, a few of us began to see lights flickering inside the darkness of the lodge. RT explained that these were illness-causing energies leaving our bodies. They were like sparks flying around and departing through the hole in the roof. This lasted for about a half hour, and then everyone became very still. Even our song master, who had been chanting most of the early part of the evening, became quiet. RT intoned a prayer in a language I had never heard before, and as he continued his chant, the inside of the lodge became lighter, as if the dawn were arriving. Yet I know it was still in the middle of the night. And then I realized that the room had not become lighter—it was the people. There was a strange luminosity coming from every person. If I focused my eyes, the light would vanish, but if I kept a soft focus, I could see a glow around each person— much like what you see around the flame in a candle when you gaze at it softly.

After the ceremony, I asked RT what I had witnessed, which others had also seen. "That was their light," he explained.

The wiracocha, I thought. The true self or soul of a person.

After the final "door," as I stood outside the lodge naked and soaked in my own sweat, I suddenly noticed that I was peeling. I had become sunburned the day before, and now that old skin was peeling off me; I could pull off strips, like a serpent shedding its skin. I looked around and saw I wasn't the only one. RT laughed.

"It's good!" he proclaimed.

I began to gulp water to rehydrate myself. I had challenged my body, which had gotten me out of my head. I felt lighter—I had probably shed some water weight, but that's not what I mean. I felt light and yet solid, too. Peaceful. Any aggression, irritation, or frustration that had weighed me down was gone.

"Yeah," I said as I looked up at the moon and watched the clouds covering it float past, freeing the moonlight to shine with intensity. "It's good. It's definitely good."

I did not feel that fleeting sense of oneness and bliss I had felt before, but what I felt was close to it. I was reminded that there are many ways to reach the same point, many maps that can take you where you wish to go, many techniques for working with the sacred, all of which can be very powerful.

Whether you decide to use the ones I offer to you here or you choose others, do the work so that your master within can awaken and we can all reap the benefits.

Prepare to Shed

We need to shed personal stories but also collective ones. We have to let go of stories of personal pain but also stories that make up the masculine, predatory mythology that have caused human beings and nature around the globe to suffer. We are going to burn these stories in the fire ceremonially, releasing the light of possibility that was born in those tragedies.

But we also need to release the stories that have become golden cages, the stories we want to hold on to because they make us feel good. We will do this so we can become empty vessels for new experiences. All of these stories will be released upon death anyway, freed to become a part of the unconscious wisdom and memory pool we all share. The detachment from them today in the fire ceremony will reveal that the void is not so empty after all: it contains tremendous potential for creation, new beliefs, ideas, and mythologies to be born.

Think about anything—a situation, a belief, a perception —that is no longer sustainable for you and that feels deadening. Maybe it's your father being neglectful, something you never forgave. Maybe it's your feeling of not fitting in or being lonely, or a story of no one truly appreciating you. Maybe it's a story of your community taking pride in being different or the "best" at something. Maybe it's a mind-set of *us* versus *them*. Release whatever stories, beliefs, or identities make you feel stuck in the past. Empty yourself of them, even if it makes you feel discombobulated at first. Trust in this transformation process.

Like the serpent sheds the skin that no longer serves her, shed stories of wounds, releasing to the fire that tale about how you are hurt by those who don't accept you as you are. Shed stories of you having been taken advantage of and disrespected. Shed stories of oppression, violence, cruelty, and exploitation of human beings anywhere. Shed the story about how your problem is that your mother still doesn't give you enough emotional support and you would have been more successful in your relationships if your parents had been better role models. Shed the story about how your marital problems have nothing to do with your parents or your grandparents. Shed the story about how the only reason you have marital problems is because your parents screwed you up.

And think about the golden stories you want to hold on to that have given you comfort. Whatever is good and true will always return to you, so don't be afraid to let them go for now. Release the story of how you are a good parent, a dedicated healer, or a wise elder. Release the story of your people triumphing over adversity. Release all stories of pride—pride in your identity, your accomplishments, your belonging to a group that has done admirable things.

Release the stories about the way you will age. Release the death that was fated for you, the tyranny of the DNA that has frightened you or made you give up on the possibility of changing your health legacy. You can burn all of this away.

Do this fire ceremony several times—and the same is true of the other fire ceremonies in this book. If you feel drawn to returning to an earlier fire ceremony, listen to your intuition and do it again until you feel ready to move on to the next fire ceremony in the sequence of serpent, jaguar, hummingbird, and eagle. You can also do these ceremonies with others, with each participant announcing what stories they are releasing.

Work within sacred space when doing the fire ceremonies in this book. You can open and close it using the invocation in the Appendix. And each time you do a sacred fire ceremony associated with serpent, jaguar, hummingbird, or eagle, have a journal or notebook and pen by your side to use for having a conversation with the power animal you encountered on the Island of Sacred Animals. It will act as a sacred witness to your work and help you awaken to your natural instincts, offering up wisdom that can assist in your evolution. Do this after your initial work with the fire—before you close sacred space.

To do the fire ceremony here and in the next chapter of this book, you will work with a pile of small sticks—even ordinary toothpicks—that you can burn in a candle or a small bowl if you cannot work outdoors in a firepit in an area where there's no chance of a spark setting off a larger fire. In the Amazon, shamans release to the fire what they call "death arrows," which are sticks into which they have blown the story and energy of whatever they wish to shed. The fire will consume and then transform these energies. Then the shaman releases life arrows of intentionality, of new dreams they hope to see made manifest.

Make sure you have something to extinguish your fire if it becomes too intense and there's a chance it might escape its container—for example, have some water to extinguish the candle you place in a bowl to work with when doing this ceremony.

Fire Ceremony for Serpent

Prepare for the fire ceremony as described avove. Then, take one stick from your pile and blow into it the feelings associated with a story that you want to shed. Start with stories you're thoroughly sick of and know are holding you back. Shed personal stories first and then collective ones, which can be harder to identify because tragic and painful stories we share with others can often give us a comfortable feeling of belonging. We bond over shared suffering, but even stories of collective pain need to go into the fire.

Shed stories that are shared by humanity. Trust that Spirit wants people to let go of those experiences, those memories of how we have hurt one another, Mother Earth, and her creatures. For example, shamans in the Andes shed the story of the Conquest and the persecution and torture of their ancestors so that the energy of those who suffered can be transformed into healing energies.

As you work your way through the pile of sticks, begin to shed the golden stories, the ones you long to cling to. Release your stories of personal accomplishments and triumphs. Then, release the stories of your community, of your country or people, that have given you pride and a sense of connection with others. Trust in this process as you release the stories one by one into a different stick for each.

Now shed your genetic legacy of developing dementia or heart disease in old age like others in your family. Shed the notion that you are doomed to develop cancer, to die in pain, to die before you have really lived.

When you have finished releasing all of these stories and your fears about them, blowing their energy into death arrows, it's time to burn it all away in the fire. You do not need to remember what each stick represents. In fact, it is best if you do not, as you have let go of these stories altogether. Hold each toothpick between your thumb and forefinger and bring the tip to the flame. Watch as it catches fire, how the flames slowly consume it and with it, your story.

When the stick is fully extinguished, pass your hand through or over the fire and touch your hand to your forehead, bringing the fire's transformative power into your third eye chakra to the wisdom center. Then do it again and bring that energy to your heart chakra, your love center. And do it a third time, bringing the energy of the fire to your belly, your second chakra, to heal your instincts and awaken your ability to manifest your highest dreams and to create. You are bringing healing energies from the vast field of possibilities into yourself.

Now that you have released your death arrows into the fire, prepare four life arrows. First, take three sticks or toothpicks and blow into the first the healing that you wish for Mother Earth, for nature, for the animals and the forests. Imagine the rivers clean, the oceans free of pollution, the air pure, and humans living in peace with nature. In the second stick, blow your intention to bring healing and peace to a loved one in need. And in the third stick, use your breath to anchor your intention to have the health and courage you need to bring beauty and peace to the world.

Then, take a fourth stick, which will be a life arrow for yourself: for growing a new body, for changing your DNA, for giving birth to a new legacy, for creating a new you who will live a new life from this day forward.

Begin to release your life arrows individually to the fire so that it can send the energy into the wind for Spirit to bring into form. In this way, you exchange the power of the stories you wish to shed for something better: the power to heal and to create something new. Share your longing, however unformed, with Spirit, knowing that your wisdom will meet with spirits in the field of possibility.

Then, call upon your power animal to help you further. Take your journal or notebook, draw a line down the center of one page, and pose the following question on the left side for your power animal to answer:

Is there anything more I need to burn away in the fire to meet the challenge of serpent and access her healing and wisdom gifts?

On the right side of the paper, write down any words and draw any image that comes to you; this is your answer. If your power animal has suggested burning away something more, create a death arrow and cast it into the fire.

Then ask your power animal the same question again, writing the answers that arise in your awareness. Then, if your power animal has suggested there is something you need to bring forth or experience to help you meet the challenge of serpent, create a life arrow for it and cast the life arrow into the fire.

If you sense you should ask more questions of your power animal, continue this conversation, blowing energy into life and death arrows to exchange energy with the fire if that's what you're guided to do. The idea is to learn from your power animal what you're resisting so that you can break out of denial about any changes you're being challenged to make. When your intuition tells you that all is good, you have done enough work for today; thank your power animal for its guidance. Close sacred space, thanking each of the directions for helping you and remembering that you're never alone in doing the work of the wisdom wheel: you are always receiving help from the invisible realms.

The Gods with a Thousand Faces and the Landscapes They Inhabit

The mythologist Joseph Campbell believed that the figures in myths were universal, that the gods with a thousand faces and myriad names were the local expression of archetypes common to all humanity. Amchi told me that the deities of every religion each inhabit a different realm in the cosmos and each tradition provides the paths and tests that will give you access to their "heavens." The image that came to my mind when he said this was that of a farmers' market: you get to go to the stalls that you want to shop at. I understood that Amchi's perspective was based on the Buddhist belief of "Buddha fields" or "pure lands" that you reincarnate into and which are under the protection of certain Buddhas. The world we are living in is one of these fields, under the protection and stewardship of Gautama Buddha.

One night as we gathered around the fire, Amchi and I began to talk about my Catholic upbringing and how the stories I had been told as a child no longer fit me. I said I wanted to make sure to not end in the Catholic track to heaven, for it required that after I died, I would have a very long wait (until the end of time) for the day of judgment and the resurrection. "Many people fear questioning what they learned in childhood," he said.

I realized that I was more interested in creating heaven on Earth today.

The Tibetan Buddhist map seemed much more comforting, where I would reincarnate shortly after leaving this body into a family that supported the dharma, the ways of wisdom. And it's said that if you became enlightened and dedicated your life to the well-being of others and the planet, you can go straight into one of the pure lands. You can choose to come back to Earth and help out if you like—that is, you can become a bodhisattva.

As we traversed the mountain paths of Nepal, I thought about the different maps we create. There are political maps showing boundaries that exist only in the minds of men, topographic maps that show the highs and lows of a landscape, and weather maps that allow you to locate the temperate zones and the desert zones. Did the maps of the Buddhists, the heavens or pure lands, intersect with those of the shamans? If the shamanic traditions of the Americas had a common origin with the Himalayan traditions 50,000 years ago, as the DNA evidence suggested, their maps of the invisible world had to intersect at some point. In the same way that you can have a chart that shows the trails and contour lines of a mountain, or another hydraulic plan that reveals the water glacial melt and the streams and lakes, and another that plots the elevations, all can describe aspects of the same mountain.

The first common point on the sacred map we can all use is the gift of serpent wisdom. It's what keeps us stuck in our culture's or community's limited stories of who we are and what we can become.

Mother of the Waters

Yakumama is the spirit of the anaconda magnified 100 times. While the anaconda can grow to a length of 10 meters, the Yakumama is gigantic. Legend says she is the mother and the guardian of all life in the Amazon, capable of summoning storms and creating deadly whirlpools in the rivers that swallow fishermen, boats and all. Loggers' invasion of the Amazon has driven the Yakumama deep into the forest, and she only appears on rare occasions to settle the score that humans have with nature, sometimes destroying entire settlements of gold miners.

I knew about the legends of the Yakumama; they are known and told by every child. I considered them fairy tales—until I met the great serpent myself.

We were in the Amazon with my friend Agustín Rivas, an extraordinary artist and sculptor (I have and cherish some of his sculptures), an excellent ayahuasca shaman, and a terrible musician who insisted on serenading us with his harmonica in every one of his ceremonies.

That night, we were working in a lodge on the shores of Lake Yarinacocha in Peru. Our maloca—a hut on stilts with a thatch roof and protected on all sides with mosquito netting—was more than 100 meters from the lakeshore, yet the Amazon had flooded its banks, as it does yearly in the rainy season. The entire campground was now part of the lake.

I had brought a group of friends and students from the United States and Europe to experience ceremonies with Agustín, who had not left the rain forest for the cities as other shamans had and still lived in the deep jungle. He could call on the spirits of the forest and the guardians of the Amazon, and they would respond to his call. He was the only shaman I have worked with that could call the jaguars to come to a ceremony—they would show up mostly in spirit form, but regularly in the flesh as well.

We were having an exquisite ceremony. When Agustín sang to the jaguars, we were able to see their eyes all around us inside the dark hut: bright yellow eyes looking deeply into our own, hundreds of them. We knew the jaguar, the totem spirit of the ayahuasca, was with us.

And then Agustín retrieved his harmonica and began to play a Christmas carol. Badly.

I have known Agustín for decades and knew that he did this to break the spell of the moment to bring people back from their journeys among the jaguars and set the tone for the next part of the ceremony. But I began to grit my teeth, not wanting to let go of the beautiful encounter I was having with the felines. And I decided to go outside to gaze at the stars.

I stepped through the screen door and onto the wooden landing, the loose planks shifting under my weight, and saw the night sky and the stars reflected in the still lake. The world was at peace, and I inhaled the moist Amazon air, breathing in the perfection of the moment. Then I opened my eyes and saw at a distance a ripple in the surface of the lake coming toward our maloca. I decided that whatever it was, I would not let it disturb the absolute peace and perfection I was experiencing. I had enough experience in the heightened states of consciousness brought about by the ayahuasca to know to relax into my breath and not let the fear hijack the moment.

As the ripple drew near, I could tell that my breathing practice was not working. I could feel the fear in my gut as my muscles tightened. And then the creature was close enough that I could see it was a giant anaconda, near 10 times my body length and as wide as a man's waist. Its scales seemed to be large blue-green turquoise stones, and when it got to the landing, it opened its mouth and showed me the ribbed roof of the inside.

Breathe, I told myself. But I could not.

Run, I could hear a part of my brain speaking. But I could not move.

I wanted to touch it, to feel its scales, to caress it. There was something terrifyingly erotic and sensual about this creature.

But I could not move. And all that I could do was to repeat the words "I am sorry."

The snake backed off and circled in the water about 30 meters away, as if waiting to see what I was going to do.

"I am sorry" in Spanish is "Lo siento." It also means "I feel it."

As I kept repenting for my life in general and a million details that flooded my mind at the moment, I began to feel her inside me. The shame I felt with the first "I am sorry" started melting and dissolving. In its place grew a sense of belonging in the rain forest, a strange sense of pleasure in my groin.

I turned to bow to the great serpent, but she was gone.

When I returned to the group, I told Agustín what I had just seen.

"It was the Yakumama," he said. "Go back outside and call her. She has a message, but be careful she does not eat you . . ."

I turned to go back outside and realized that my entire body was shaking. I could not move. I dropped to the floor and covered my head with my poncho. Even though the night was warm, I had the chills and my jaw was moving uncontrollably. And I realized I had wet my pants.

Agustín came over and shook my shoulder. "You must go back," he said.

"Go away," I said—and asked him to play his harmonica so I could break this spell.

The next morning, Agustín explained that the river people, the ones that live inside the river, not the humans at the edge of the river, were called the Yacuruna. The Anaconda people, ancient beings that prefer the deep waters of the river, will occasionally mate with a human female. Or they will take a shaman to mate with one of their own and return him a week later.

"This is pretty far-out stuff," I said. "You don't really expect me to believe this, do you?" Invisible beings mating with humans . . .

"Why not?" he asked. "What about Mary and God?"

"But that's different!" I protested.

He nodded. "Of course it is. Of course."

The serpent lets you shed that which prevents you from discovering what else you could experience. It lets you see the bigger picture: the interconnectedness among people, among experiences, among mythologies. It lets you see that when we are in conflict with each other, we're in conflict with ourselves, and vice versa—so there's no need to be overwhelmed by the thought of healing the world. Such a seemingly massive undertaking is in our power because we heal the world through healing ourselves.

When we stop perceiving the feminine and sensuality as evil, when we reclaim the parts of ourselves we keep buried in the shadow realms and embody our passion, we will find ways to work with the Kundalini energy that serves both ourselves and others. And then, just as the butterfly beating its wings can cause a cleansing storm on the other side of the world that eases a drought, we can trust that our choices and our healing make a difference.

CHAPTER 6

JAGUAR WISDOM
(THE WEST)

We were in a mud-and-stone hall at Charang, just outside Ghar Gumba, the temple of Guru Rinpoche that legend says 200 men built during the day only to have their work taken down in the evening by 200 demons. Guru Rinpoche had to brandish his ceremonial knife, known as a phurba, to tame them. He had first tried fighting but found that when he tore off the limb of one demon, another would spring up from the spot where it had landed, so he had to turn them into allies and protectors of the dharma, the wisdom teaching.

Great metaphors for psychologists, I thought. We are trained to dig up old wounds and dissect them, but from every painful event we find and try to do away with, another one springs forth. I had become frustrated with psychotherapy years ago because of the exhausting and seemingly endless process that can turn you into a lifelong patient with a perfect understanding of why you were so dysfunctional but no ability to change it.

On the trail today, we crossed a mountain pass at a 13,000-foot altitude. At the top were a pile of stones the height of a person placed there ceremonially by ancient pilgrims and traders along the Silk Road who had rested at this very place. The pile was adorned with tattered and torn prayer flags tied to a high pole that rose from the center of the mound of stones. When we reached it, we each said a prayer of thanks and left a stone as our predecessors had. Then we found a spot protected from the wind where we rested and dug into our trail mix. But Marcela, who was always the disciplined one, remained by the cairn, holding a stone tenderly in her hands, blowing into it softly, oblivious to the biting cold wind.

"Ah, a true practitioner!" exclaimed Joan. I looked at Marcela in admiration. Once again, she was pushing herself to do what she had come here to do: experience moments of sacred connection even when the going was rough.

Later that night when we were in our tent in Ghar Gumba, I recalled how many opportunities I had missed to pray wholeheartedly at sacred sites. Too easily seduced by my bag of trail mix or the banter of friends.

I would change that.

Tucked into my sleeping bag, I could feel the warmth radiating from Marcela's sleeping bag next to mine. I prayed myself to sleep, reciting the mantra of Guru Rinpoche that Amchi had taught us, the prayer that Buddhist masters said can clear away obstacles and reconnect us in body, speech, and mind to the divine: "Om Ah Hum Vajra Guru Padma Siddhi Hum."

I woke up having dreamed of the snow lion, a magnificent creature with a red mane, which ran toward me and leaped over me at the very last moment. I remember looking up and seeing its underbelly. It was a female, with six nipples.

And I heard her speak to me, saying, "I will show you the middle way."

I shared the dream with Carol, hoping to get her interpretation, since she was our expert on Bön Buddhism. "The snow lion is the symbol of Shakyamuni Buddha," she explained. "She is fearless, and her milk is said to heal the body and soul."

"What about the middle way?" I asked. I knew the Buddha had been an ascetic, depriving himself of all worldly things *including food and nearly dying. He was saved by a maiden who nursed him back to health with yak milk. It was then that he decided that the way of extreme abstinence would not lead him to the freedom he sought. The lesson? Don't go to this extreme. But we should not go to the other extreme either: overindulging in sensual pleasure. The middle way between those extremes is best.*

"The middle way is to follow the Buddha's path to liberation," Carol replied.

Four truths. So simple: As the Buddhists say, in life, we suffer. Suffering is caused by attachment. Shedding attachments is the way to alleviate suffering. Shedding attachments happens when we follow the Eightfold Path of Buddhism, a list of "right ways" to interact with yourself, others, and the world around you.

Yes, *I said to myself,* there is a middle way if you're willing to love yourself as you are.

I thought about how the value of punishing yourself had been deeply ingrained in me by my Catholic upbringing. I'd been doing that mentally for a long time. I realized the snow lion dream was telling me to accept who I am and to drink from the milk of the wisdom of the wild cats, of the lioness, the greatest of all. We are here to love and heal, not to compare wounds and rank our level of suffering or turn our pain into a fetish that makes us feel special and superior. Today, Amchi is set to lead us in a Medicine Buddha initiation to heal the mental poisons within us. Great timing, *I thought.* So much of my pain is self-inflicted. I can use that initiation.

In Western culture, we value the mind for making sense of the world and our experiences. But while we might think we possess our mind, our mind can possess us. The challenge of jaguar in the wisdom wheel does not require you to cut your brain out of your head or make it your enemy. It requires you to optimize your brain, detoxifying it and upgrading it so that you can attain the wisdom gift of jaguar: the conquering of your primal and existential fears, especially your fear of death and your fear of being hurt by love. It's fear that keeps you attached to things you need to let die. It's fear that keeps you from moving forward into unfamiliar territory with the ease of a jaguar exploring the unknown. It's fear that causes you to focus on the power to dominate others and get them to follow your will when it's the power to collaborate and co-create that you've been missing—the power of the divine feminine.

The Tibetan female deities, known as the dakinis, are often depicted holding a moon-shaped knife in one hand and a cup made from a skull in the other. I always found these images intriguing and wondered why they were so prevalent in the Himalayan region. When I began to learn the way of the jaguar medicine with Amazon shamans who employed ayahuasca—the vine of death—to facilitate their journeying, I started looking into the dakinis. Dakinis represent the union of wisdom, which is represented by the skull, and skillful means, represented by the knife. These deities also represent separating from worldly attachments—what the brain perceives and desires—to achieve enlightenment.

In the world of science, we identify with the mind and with the brain, the seat of consciousness. I wondered: Did the dakinis suggest that you had to do away with your brain altogether to attain enlightenment? I remembered reading how the ancient Egyptians mummified every organ in the body so the deceased pharaoh could gain use of them in the afterlife—except for the brain. They drained the brain out of the skull by sticking two straws up the mummy's nostrils.

The brain and the mind can get in the way of where you want to go.

It's the jaguar that gives us the power and courage to take the leap out of our need to feel safe and secure in the world and trust in the unseen. And it's the jaguar that is our ally and companion as we descend into the darkness of

Mother Earth, entering the belly of the divine feminine, to heal those parts of us that are encased in pain.

Here in the dark womb, we discover the love of the eternal mother, the one who will never leave us, who will hold us until the end of our days and offer us resources and allies if we surrender our fear and trust in her loving, healing ways. She will offer us the seeds for growth and limitless possibilities for finding and generating love. When these seeds germinate, we will be able to stop expecting the people we love to love us back exactly as we want them to. Then we will become love itself.

Jaguar's gift to us is this: our fear of disconnection through romantic breakups, estrangements, or even death will be soothed by a faith that love will find ways to renew itself in myriad forms. As humans, we are social creatures who need others—who need to feel we can be fully ourselves, vulnerable yet safe, with another human being. I'll never forget the intense feeling of connection I had after coming out of isolation with Marcela during the pandemic when I saw an old friend and hugged him. Before, it would have been an ordinary greeting. Now I felt its power and was reminded of jaguar's lesson: love is everywhere, expressing itself over and over again. There's no need to fear that it will disappear.

Banishing the Big Fear

We fear the death of the body because we assume it means the death of who we are, of all that we have accomplished, experienced, loved, and believed. Will we disappear when our brains cease to function and our hearts stop beating? Will our memories be erased? Will those left behind remember us? For how long? It's a challenge to release the biggest fear of all: the fear of death and the loss of the self and all we know and love. The illusion of immortality is strong when we are young. As we lose people we love and our bodies begin to show signs of aging, it's harder to avoid the realization that we are in the last lap of life and that it will soon come to an abrupt and not very elegant end.

I remember as a child saying a prayer my grandmother taught me: "If I shall die before I wake, I pray the Lord my soul to take." I lost count of how many nights I waited anxiously for the sunrise to make sure I did not die in my sleep. And on top of that, I was terrified that if I had to pray to the Lord to take my soul, what other predators were around that could abscond with it? What if the Lord was off that night or on holiday? Then who would take my soul—and where?

You are invited to do the emotionally challenging work of facing your mortality so you can free yourself from the haunting fear of losing the self that colors your life and limits you. The Tibetan Buddhists call this the practice of impermanence. Time passes by quickly; opportunities come and go. The task is twofold. First, you allow yourself to feel your fear and grief as you face the undeniable reality that you will at some point lose everything and everyone you love. Second, you must turn your mourning into a practice of being infinitely present and grateful for the moment at hand. Ever-present awareness of impermanence frees you from the primal grip that the fear of death and loss of self has had over you. It prevents you from finding yourself on your deathbed experiencing the common regret of not having prioritized spending time with those you love. As we grow older, the children's prayer of "if I shall die before I wake" no longer seems strange. We weigh the odds of suddenly dying in our sleep, and then we tell ourselves that there's no need to get morbid about it: we'll be here a very long time, and we'll be just fine. But will we?

Deep in our hearts, we remain concerned. While we have banished our fear of death to the depths of our unconscious, it casts its long shadow over us and is ready to arise at a moment's notice when we are reminded of our mortality. But if we could release this primordial fear, coax it out from its hiding place and bathe it in the sunlight, we would be primed for a new appreciation of each moment and the possibilities it brings.

One of those possibilities is that perhaps you can live longer than you believe you can, and in good health. It's curious how the increase in maximum life span has resulted in many more years of being sick and bedridden rather than skiing in the Alps into your 90s. We can give up our habit of denying the effects of lifestyle choices and use what we know about the brain and our energy field to change the expression of our DNA and live even longer healthier.

Another possibility is to quiet your fearful, primitive brain so you can begin to smell the flowers—to appreciate the next breath and see opportunities hidden from those not living in the present moment and who are regretting the past or worrying about the future or both. To me, the mandate to "awaken, awaken" means to engage the more evolved regions of the brain, the neocortex and prefrontal lobes, so you can more easily practice fearlessness and see clearly when the path to what you desire is obscured by darkness. In my earlier books, I have written extensively on the neuroscience of enlightenment and about the diet and lifestyle that can support this awakening. Meditation, ritual, ceremony, and time spent in nature can quiet the primitive brain that wants you to fret about yesterday, second-guess yourself, and stress out about what might happen tomorrow. There are other payoffs to doing the work of the jaguar— possibilities you can access that will bring more love into your life. The work of the West gives you the power to heal the sense of loss, hurt, and suffering you inflict on yourself and others in your love relationships. You will be able to see what you are willing to accept and find the courage to walk away from what's unacceptable.

And the work of jaguar, which teaches you to be present in the moment, frees you from nostalgia and conforming to stale norms about what people in your stage of life are supposed to do, think, and feel. Even when we haven't a single gray hair, we often assume we have used up all of the opportunities we'll ever get in life. Death is also the loss of vitality, and it can happen incrementally in small ways. You might not even realize this is happening. Shamans say the real death is not the death of the body but the death of one's innocence and openness to the mystery of life. It's the death that takes you away bit by bit as you lose your optimism, leaving you with a sense that you've learned all there is to learn and now you're just in a holding pattern, hoping to remain for as long as you can before death comes to claim you. It's the death of hope for the future, however short your life may end up being. Confront your fears and you will recognize that your wiracocha, the authentic you, will continue to exist.

When a jaded, pessimistic attitude sets in, people sometimes take comfort in nostalgia. They forget about the bad times and only remember the good old days, endlessly reminiscing about a golden era before everything became fouled up and awful. To remain in this comforting state of mind, they avoid trying anything new. Spending time around them can be exhausting and draining, but some fearful part of you that has noticed your first wrinkle or that your knees don't hold up for long walks like they used to may be tempted to join in and keep them company.

Other people who become cynical become closed off to exploration, bitter, and even irritable. They go on relentlessly about their aches and pains and past hurts and have trouble feeling gratitude for all that is right with their lives. They might not realize they can look forward to a future that they help shape for the good of all. They can choose to become an 85-year-old who is developing an app or solving problems regarding climate change and sustainability or beginning a new romance. But they have to choose surrender so the new adventure can begin.

Surrender to Uncertainty

As we face global challenges, more of us are becoming concerned about where society is headed and what we can do to avoid disastrous scenarios in the years to come. For example, scroll through a newsfeed on your phone and you're almost certain to read about a death somewhere. Death is a part of life, and uncertainty about what the future holds for us can strike terror in our hearts. The work of the West is to surrender to this uncertainty and let go of the assumptions and beliefs that zap us of our life force and creativity and make us cynical and wooden. We do this to free ourselves to embark on a new adventure and toward a new destiny for ourselves and others.

The ancients understood the power of jaguar wisdom, which gives us the courage to practice beginner's mind, to greet the ordinary with childlike wonder, and to dive into a vast pool of yet-unexplored wisdom. You will have to open up to the mystery of the unknown, jump off the cliff into the mist, and trust that you will land on solid ground on the other side of the abyss and not fall into the depths below.

The mists I speak of are like the mists of Avalon that part only when we embrace our innocence and awe, when we open to wisdom beyond our own, beyond experiences in the visible world. In the lore of the Andes, there was a golden city called Vilcabamba, the Sacred Place, which has over time receded into the mists and is no longer reachable by ordinary mortals. The shamans say that the jaguar symbolizes a rainbow bridge from our world to the invisible one, to the mythic Vilcabamba where we can tap into the wisdom of sages past and future. One of my Andean mentors, Don Manuel Quispe, had explained to me that the flag of the Inca is the rainbow because we humans are made from light and earth. We don't realize it because our light, our wiracocha or true self, becomes obscured by disappointment and despair. The goal of the shaman is to release herself from the grip of fear and restore her light so that she can cross the rainbow bridge at the moment of her death—walk over the back of the rainbow jaguar that links our visible world to the invisible world. With her light restored, her fear of death gone, she can do great healing and perform sacred ceremonies, more powerfully than ever before.[1]*

Descend into the Darkness and Befriend Your Demons

In the patriarchal view of the world, we are separate from Mother Earth and her nurturing care. We have Father Sun, the light, to illuminate what is before us and around us, but if something frightens us, we try to leave it in the shadows so that it's easier to carry on. We learned to move forward, ready to slay enemies that stand in the way of personal progress and achievement and ignoring any unhealed wounds we have suffered. We face external challenges and try not to become distracted by internal ones.

Challenges can bring out the best in us, and ultimately, they are unavoidable. However, while you can gain praise for being a brave warrior out in the world who is unafraid to draw his sword in the face of danger, you are going to

---

[1] *Imagine my surprise when the head priest at the Bön monastery told us that in that very temple, a great teacher had attained what he called "rainbow body." I asked what he meant by that, and the priest explained that teacher had become awakened, realizing his undying nature as a luminous being attached to a biological body.

set aside that mythic story. Instead, consciously choose to go on a journey that might bring no glory at all. You will be spiraling down into the darkness of the mother womb, dealing with the demons within—which isn't as attractive a goal as slaying dragons and proving your mettle to admiring observers.

And you're not going to slay the demons you find. You're not going to have a sword at your side. You're going to befriend the demons using wisdom and skillful means so they hand over their gifts to you freely. Like the nagas, they will resist doing so unless you're willing to face the challenges they present to you.

Mahatma Gandhi was once asked how he planned to end British colonial rule in India when the Indian people were clearly outmanned and outgunned. His reply was that he would get the British to leave on their own. What some thought was a lunatic plan turned out to be a brilliant one. It wasn't as if Gandhi and his followers presented a rational, civil explanation for why the British should leave, to which the British replied, "Why, of course! What were we thinking occupying your land? We'll pack our bags right now and get out of your way." Gandhi understood the potential in battling through nonviolent resistance that appealed to the better selves of the enemy. Nonviolent resistance did not mean the Indian people suffered no violence or death, but they may have suffered fewer deaths than they would have in a protracted war in which they were ill-matched against the British empire.

In the Americas, we are so well versed in the metaphors of war and battle that it can be hard to remember the power of getting others to change their minds and awaken to a higher way of thinking. But when the odds are not in our favor, it's an opportunity to employ the tools that can draw on the deep wisdom in the invisible realm and tap into a mind that is willing to co-create anew with Spirit.

When we give up the fear that makes us treat life as if it were a battleground, others are likely to be inspired to do so as well. Then we don't have to try to force others to see things our way. Rather, we can see each other as potential collaborators. To make this happen, we have to turn our demons into allies. We have to start feeding them with our love and understanding rather than trying to defeat them.

The darkness you may encounter in doing the work of the West is the fruitful darkness within the Earth, in the realm of the lower world where the secrets of the past and the hurtful memories dwell. What seem to be demons intent on harming you will turn out to be parts of yourself that need love, but that first need to be acknowledged. Like with Guru Rinpoche, whatever temple you build in the world during the day, your demons will come out in the dark of the night to tear them down—that is, until you befriend them. There is no way to destroy or "macho" your way through them. They stand strong, blocking your way until you put down your sword and open up to learning what they have to offer you.

Exploring the darkness where our personal and collective demons dwell isn't exactly an attractive pursuit, but all of us have to do it at some point regardless of our resistance. It's best not to save that moment to the end of your life. You don't want to spend your last days reminiscing how the past could have been different and seeking atonement for all your misdeeds.

Haven't we all experienced frustration and resentment when we feel anger, hurt, or grief and someone tells us to look on the bright side? Resist anyone else's urging to remain light and cheerful. Overzealous positivity is often rooted in a fear of exploring one's own darkness, and it can be contagious. This is magical thinking, and it is very different from the work of the shaman. If you give into it, blinded by the light of a fake positive attitude, afraid to go deep into your past, you will skip the important healing and liberating work of spotting and befriending your demons.

Your demons might include your unwillingness to risk offending someone as you pursue your own path, fear of being true to yourself, or perhaps shame at having failed at achieving a goal or winning someone's approval. These "demons" are not the events that happened but the attitudes and beliefs that you adopted as a way of coping with the hurt. They hide from your conscious awareness but continue to influence you, scaring you into remaining on your current path despite your dissatisfaction.

As an explorer in the darkness, you are going deep within to love the parts of yourself that were shamed. You will experience the hurt, the anger, the sadness over what you left behind when you decided it was better to "get on with it" than remain present with what was happening and how it was tormenting you. This is psychological work that you do alone. It will be unpleasant, but it is important. The challenge is to be present with the ugliness of the root system, the worms, and the sense of oppression beneath the dirt that can feel as if it's trying to keep you from living.

The demons of your emotions that are hidden in the darkness have important lessons for you. Be willing to lean into the discomfort of looking honestly at yourself, your choices, and your past. In response, these demons will offer nutrients for the hidden seeds that promise to push through the darkness and allow you to grow something new and glorious. In other words, it's time to turn that old crap into compost so the seeds of change can begin to sprout.

In the darkness, you will encounter that great pain that you have carried since you were little and that your mother and her mother before her also carried to their last days of life and find that it becomes the source of your compassion and generosity. Its gift and lessons are to feel empathy and express kindness to others because you know what it is like to hurt. Then, as your deep wound begins to heal, your power and energy will grow. You will experience the enormous potential for transformation with the help of the nurturing, loving force of the divine feminine who surrounds you and supports you as you explore new territory like the jaguar does.

You do not have to eradicate the old, painful memories. Remember that many are not even yours: they belong to generations past and to our collective history. You can transform them and how they live within you, integrating them into who you are today and who you are becoming. The demon of hurt can become an angel of truth. The demon of pride can become an angel of generosity. And while the events of years ago caused your heart to break and your life to contract, you can learn to become a bold explorer once again because of this healing work.

You can recover innocence and a beginner's mind when you befriend the demons that arose when you were wounded long ago. Then, instead of projecting onto a present situation old notions about how you can't trust others, or how you will never be loved the way you long to be loved, you will come to it with an open heart. You will extend trust despite all the betrayals, offer love despite all the losses, and become curious and take a risk despite all the failures that came with a heavy price.

In this dark womb of the mother, you'll discover that you are safe after all. You don't need to fight anything outside of you or fear monsters in the mist. You don't have to deny parts of yourself to avoid pain. You can reclaim them, repurpose them, and weave them into your being so you can become whole again. You simply need to love that which hurts inside you.

But your brain is programmed for fear, so you must retrain it. You have to take that knife from the hand of the dakini and slice open your own mind.

The shamans of the Andes had a similar knife, which they called a *tumi*. A tumi is a half-moon-shaped ceremonial blade sometimes made from precious metals that is found in ancient burial sites. Archaeologists have no idea what practical use these tools had. Perhaps they were representing that slicing through the dark that keeps us separated from Vilcabamba, the Sacred Place between the worlds. I am convinced that accessing it requires losing your mind to come to your senses. Your natural senses have the power to reveal a different reality from the one you are currently experiencing.

The Mind and Its Power to Generate Reality

Jaguar medicine—jaguar wisdom—is the cure for the mind-trap that keeps us in safe territory, afraid to find out what happens when we leave the familiar. However, each of us was born with the potential to explore new worlds. It's our birthright, encoded in our DNA and activated by the life force that gives birth to a brain capable of creating psychosomatic disease, or, alternatively, creating health and well-being. Our brains can create an illusion that is just as convincing as reality. Ask any actor if they are actually feeling sad when playing a character who has just lost a loved one, and they'll say yes; it's a genuine emotion they've tricked themselves into feeling and expressing. The tears are real even if the movie plot and character are fiction. Any of us can conjure up thoughts or emotions that cue our bodies to respond appropriately.

Also, when we sleep, we dream—and those dreams feel very real. Are they? Given that it is so easy to get the brain to experience the imaginary as real, like an actor or a magician does, is the brain foolish, or is it brilliant? If the body can respond to the reality created within the mind, shouldn't we appreciate that ability and use it to our benefit?

According to the shamans, we can work with the field of infinite possibilities that we are part of, and with serpent, jaguar, hummingbird, and eagle medicine, make the impossible possible. We can co-create a world that's preferable to the one we will likely experience in the future as humanity slides along the slippery slope toward extinction.

It's said that the balams, or jaguar priests of the Maya, could travel freely between the visible and invisible worlds, the realms of the living and the dead. I believe that the day has come when we need to relearn how to do this so we can conjure into being a new world, as the old one is on the verge of collapse. But the conjuring we need is not going to come around through whimsical wishing or waving a magic wand. It will require enough people with brains functioning at the highest levels to infuse the field of reality we all share with a new common purpose. We will have to discover a consciousness different from the familiar one.

Get Ready to Experience a Higher State of Consciousness

To experience the higher level of consciousness I'm talking about, you must use the most recently evolved part of your brain: your prefrontal cortex (located behind your forehead). To prepare your brain to awaken this ability and let you experience oneness with Spirit and all of creation, you have to calm the region of the brain where the fear response lives: the limbic brain. Otherwise, it will convince you to procrastinate, distract yourself, and avoid the difficult work of exploring who you are and who you can become, what you have lost and what you can gain, and what you can do to contribute to the evolutionary process we are all undergoing.

One of the functions of the prefrontal cortex is to inhibit the ancient limbic brain, which lives in fear and scarcity.

This brain prefers its own opinions to the facts and cannot be persuaded by evidence to the contrary. It's in this part of our brain where we experience the fight-or-flight-or-freeze stress response: the activation of the HPA (hypothalamic-pituitary-adrenal) axis.

The limbic brain's stress response occurs not only when we fear for our lives but when we fear for our reputations: the fierce beast about to gore you that has your heart pumping turns out to be your boss accusing you of not being sufficiently productive and efficient. The fear you experience when faced with a threat you cannot fight or flee from causes your sympathetic nervous system to kick into action and freeze in the "on" position. Instead of helping you remain safe from bodily harm, your nervous system ends up wreaking havoc, damaging the very structures you need to overcome a threat.

When you are in fight-or-flight-or-freeze, stress hormones flood your bloodstream. Initially, that's a good thing because it offers your body the energy to flee danger or put up a fierce fight. Over time, as the sympathetic nervous system continues pumping adrenaline, the result is cellular damage in every organ.

External toxins that have made their way into your body, along with dead cells and natural waste products from metabolism and the breakdown of hormones, begin to build up inside the brain. This overloads your body's detox systems and compromises your immune system. Your brain and body become sluggish—frozen, so to speak. Meanwhile, toxins that normally get cycled out of the body are now stored in body fat, which starts to affect your brain's ability to grow new neurons. Remember that the brain is 70 percent fat, and if you're going to store toxins temporarily, it's not the ideal place.

To stop this harmful cascade of biochemical responses to fear and stress, you must learn how to quiet the sympathetic nervous system and turn on the parasympathetic nervous system that allows you to relax and repair your body at a cellular level—and do this often. Meditation can be very effective, especially if you take more time exhaling the air you inhale than you took breathing it in.

The exercise below was inspired by a lesson my mentors in the Amazon rain forest taught me that while the jaguar has no predators, sometimes it becomes so frightened that it climbs a tree and will not come down. It needs to relax, to remember that it is safe in the darkness and that there will always be food available and territory to explore. We too can become like the cat in the tree, convinced that we're in danger when we're not. Even if we try to talk ourselves out of feeling fearful, our nervous system remains in freeze mode. At the physical level, we call this chronic stress.

Humans are the only animal on the planet that cannot reset their stress response. The deer that freezes in the headlights goes into an autonomic reset as soon as you drive away. A quiver begins at the tip of its nose that goes all the way through its body and out its tail, and then the deer goes back to being at ease, grazing lazily. But human brains are too complex. We talk ourselves into holding on to our fear—and the internal reality created by our thoughts keeps us living in what we believe to be a dangerous, predatory world, a belief for which we find confirmation every day.

Use this exercise to turn on the parasympathetic nervous system and come to your higher senses. It will also entrain your heartbeat to that of Mother Earth, helping you feel a connection to her and her loving comfort.

Connecting to the Heartbeat of Mother Earth

Start by sitting in a comfortable position, breathing in as you silently count to three. Hold your breath for a second, and then exhale to a count of five. This pattern of breathing cues your sympathetic nervous system to relax.

Then, place your right palm over your heart center and your left palm over your right hand. Notice whether you can feel the beating of your heart. Now move your right hand onto your belly, just below your navel over your second chakra, where you have an invisible umbilical cord that stretches from your body to Mother Earth. Imagine you can feel your heartbeat with your left hand as you tune into your body's great drummer. Imagine too that you can feel the heartbeat of Mother Earth. Let her tune your heart to hers, as if you were a newborn baby lying on your mother's breast. Let your second chakra know that everything is going to be okay, that all is well, for your mother is looking after you. Instruct your second chakra to relax. You are safe and will continue to be safe.

Then, bring your palms together at your heart again and thank the Great Mother for holding you sweetly.

You can also do this exercise with a loved one. Have the person lie down on their back, and slide your left hand, palm up, between the shoulder blades, where the heart chakra is located. (Remember, chakras are accessed through the front or the back of the body.) Engage your imagination and feel the heartbeat of Mother Earth. Now place your right hand underneath their second chakra, in the sacral area. Bring the heartbeat of the Earth into your own heart and then into your partner's through your hand. Speak to their second chakra like you would to a scared child, reassuring it, "You'll be okay. You're safe. It's okay. Mother's here. All is well." Do this until you can feel your loved one relaxing and breathing deeply.

> When you're finished, bring your palms to your heart center and thank Mother Earth. She has brought the jaguar down to a lower branch, helped it relax with only the tip of its tail twitching, and it now can observe the world and recognize that all is well.

A locked fight-or-flight system causes us to have trouble sleeping, and quality sleep is necessary to restore our bodies and ensure cellular repair. Connecting with the heartbeat of Mother Earth allows us to become and radiate peace, flipping a switch to turn on the parasympathetic nervous system, coaxing the jaguar out of the tree. It becomes easier to sleep well.

Another way to coax the jaguar out of the tree (to turn on the parasympathetic nervous system) is to change your eating patterns to support the optimal functioning of your brain.

Cultivate a Fat and Happy Brain

Our brains are made up largely of fats, and good fats like those you find in avocados and olive oil are their ideal food. However, the brain also runs on sugars, which are simple carbohydrates. Our sugar-rich diets cue our brains to burn the inferior fuel. The sugar-fed brain finds it nearly impossible to eliminate toxins and waste products such as protein tangles, which can accelerate the onset of dementia. When you're in chronic fight-or-flight and feeding your brain on sweets, you cue yourself to experience mental confusion, forgetfulness, and a habit of letting the emotional center of the brain generate fear and anxiety.

Fortunately, dietary changes including supplementing with DHA (an omega-3 fatty acid essential for health) and intermittent fasting can repair your hippocampus and coax your brain to run on healthy fats from nuts, seeds, avocados, and meat and fish from animals that lived the way they were designed to: roaming or swimming freely in their natural environment. By avoiding processed foods such as refined sugars and simple carbohydrates, limiting fruit to its natural form (high in fiber), and restricting grains (consuming organically grown whole grains in moderation), you can help your brain repair and reset. Eating a primarily plant-based diet will prevent cellular damage and buildup of cellular waste in the brain and body. If you don't eat fish, think about adding that to your plate. Fish is brain food—it has healthy omega-3 fats that tend to be scarce in the Western diet, which features unhealthy fats and excessive amounts of omega-6 fats.

Intermittent fasting can teach your brain to switch over to burning fat for fuel. It's as simple as not eating after 6 P.M. and waiting until 11 A.M. to break your fast. Your body will draw upon stored fats to feed the brain. Be patient in the changeover and work with a nutritionist during this process. And as you make these changes, be prepared for some headaches and physical discomfort that will, in time, give way to feeling much more energized and clearheaded.

Once you have retrained your brain and nervous system, it becomes far easier to let go of the fears that hold you back from going forth adventurously like the jaguar exploring the rain forest. Then you have to be aware of when you're slipping back into old ways and make new, conscious decisions not to move backward.

Take the Leap

As you can see, to metaphorically "eat from the fruit of the tree of life everlasting" and live longer and more healthfully than you're programmed to requires physical changes. You can learn much from those who live in the blue zones, places in the world where an unusual number of people age health-fully. These are places where community connections are maintained—including intergenerational ones. The younger people learn from the elders and vice versa. Elders under-stand they need to be open to new ideas and ways.

The blue zones are also places where people understand the value of supporting the arthritic old man who can barely walk and the energetic younger people who can be active all day long and still pull an all-nighter. All stages of life have value. All perspectives offer something to the conversation around the fire. But at the end of the day, you have to be open to the wisdom of those around you, the gifts of those you may have overlooked. You have to be open to new ways of thinking and perceiving so that love can flourish.

Doing the inner work of the jaguar, of befriending your demons and bestowing love on them so you release your-self from the grip of your fears, makes it easier to be com-passionate toward the pontificators, the braggarts, and the insufferable know-it-alls because you know you've been like them at times. Conversations and problem-solving become easier when you are honest about your own failings and able to laugh at yourself. When you're no longer afraid of feeling foolish or inconsequential, you will develop a healthy rela-tionship with your fear: it can guide you without unneces-sarily setting off a fight-or-flight-or-freeze response. You can let go of your feelings of scarcity and your fear that if you don't hold on to what you have, you will fall apart.

Be brave: step into the mist.

Use the jaguar fire ceremony often to release the fear within you and regain your vitality, your courage, your curi-osity, and your openness to explore uncharted territory. As I said before, it's best to work within sacred space using the invocation (found in the Appendix) and have a journal and pen by your side to use for having a conversation with your power animal after the fire ceremony.

Fire Ceremony for Jaguar

Prepare for the ceremony according to the instructions given for the fire ceremony for serpent, which you learned about in the last chapter (page 83). This time, however, you will start by blowing into a death arrow any regret you feel about your romantic relationships that makes it difficult for you to love wholeheartedly and trust in the healing power of love. You want to do this so you can release the pain and embody the lessons learned. The person that you felt abandoned or betrayed you, the one that deceived you, the one that broke their promises to you, or the one that you hurt? Name this person aloud so that you acknowledge the lingering power of that memory. Then, cast the stick holding the energy of that love relationship into the fire.

Next, create a death arrow for your fears about being disconnected from others, from love, for good. Cast it into the fire so that you transform it.

Then, create a death arrow for your fears about repeating the emotional and lifestyle patterns in your family that lead to illness and even death. You might let go of heartache and heart disease or of being consumed with anger, or even cancer.

If you don't know what family patterns you are repeating that might manifest as illness or death, speak out loud the words "I release to the fire the death I am likely to experience because of my genetics and my choices." Blow that into a death arrow for the fire to transform.

Any cynical belief that it's too late to change now, that a certain type or timing of death is inevitable for you, needs to be released. If you have a belief like this, take at least one stick, one death arrow, to use in bringing that belief to the fire to burn it up. Speak your belief out loud. For example, "I release to the fire the death I think I can't avoid because it's too late to change my life or habits."

Next, you will create life arrows.

Blow into the first life arrow your desire to explore new possibilities about the choices you make day to day that affect your health, well-being, and relationships. Are you ready to love more freely, without conditions and preconceived notions about the form love takes? Are you ready to adopt new beliefs about your health and how you will age and die so you can grow a new body? Are you ready to live a more enlivened life so that you can feel a sense of vitality again? Set an intention and blow it into the life arrow. Then, release it to the fire.

Remember, each life arrow that contains your intentions for living differently, for loving differently, for exploring who you might become, will be transformed by the fire into pure energy for change.

Finally, blow into a stick the intention to die without fear or regrets, with no words left unsaid or deeds not done. Place it in the fire for transformation.

Using a journal and a pen, have and record a conversation with your power animal to see if there are any more death and life arrows you need to create before thanking it and closing sacred space.

CHAPTER 7

HUMMINGBIRD WISDOM
(THE NORTH)

Ghar Gumba is an unassuming temple in the middle of a vast and unforgiving sea of sand. The caretaker who came to the door was an old man with one of his front teeth missing and a well-worn monk's robe, the red faded and cloth thinned from too many washings at the river. Recognizing Amchi, he opened the temple for us. Even though there were no other visitors, more than two dozen butter lamps were burning, casting their pale shadows over the tankas and statues of the Buddha, including one of Guru Rinpoche.

Amchi invited Marcela and me, together with our friend Stephan, to visit the secret collection of ancient paintings of the mahasiddhas: the great teachers who had achieved enlightenment and developed extraordinary powers, like the ability to fly. I have known Stephan for decades—we are like brothers—but I did not know that for many years, he had been practicing a mantra of Guru Rinpoche that he had been told could dispel obstacles. I had been given the same mantra by a master shaman who was also a Buddhist Lama. I was told it could summon power and protection to oneself, but even more importantly, it could help you cross safely through the bardo, the intermediate place between life and death, encountered after this life ends.

"Om Ah Hung Vajra Guru Pema Siddhi Hung."

It's said you cannot give this mantra away to someone else until you have recited it 100,000 times. I am sure I have done at least that many.

By the main altar, we entered through a side door that seemed to have been designed for very short people: we had to hunch over to get through. Then, we followed Amchi through a maze of passages up to a second story where the floor had partially collapsed onto the level below.

"This is it," Amchi said as we reached a dimly lit hall with dozens of paintings no larger than a notebook hanging on the walls. Ghastly beings with tongues of fire and sublime meditators were levitating above the clouds.

"Did they have any help with the flying?" I asked Amchi. I had been reading Ian Baker's The Heart of the World, *about his travels in Tibet, including a foray in the Pemako and a stretch of the Tsangpo River never explored by Westerners that lay in a gorge three times the depth of the Grand Canyon. Pemako was said to be the site of a legendary secret kingdom—a lost paradise. Baker and his group of explorers discovered patches of psilocybin mushrooms growing in the wild. Could these psychedelics have been the key to the mahasiddhas flying, much like the amanita muscaria mushroom allowed the wise women of Northern Europe to fly on their legendary broomsticks?*

Amchi did not think so. "Only meditation," he said.

As a doctor of Tibetan medicine, Amchi knows his medicinal plants and herbs, and he certainly has run across the mind-altering plants, even if he has not tried them. I have tasted enough of the various mind-enhancing potions of the Amazon to know spirit-flight and how one can feel like an eagle flying above the clouds. I even became a condor once and soared above ancient

Inca temples. I felt confident that the monks who had explored realms of the soul and become such consummate cartographers of the invisible world knew psychedelics.

"Only meditation," Amchi repeated.

"Okay," I said. "Let's go meditate. I want to try to fly."

We made our way back out through the maze to the temple. Once inside, we saw Joan and the rest of our group were waiting for Amchi to lead us in a Medicine Buddha empowerment ceremony.

Avoiding the pillars that supported the roof structure, which seemed a bit precarious, we took places on the floor. As I settled in, I noticed that my cushion was right below the statue of Guru Rinpoche.

Joan looked around to make sure we were all paying attention, as we were looking to her to help us understand what we were seeing. "The Medicine Buddha," she began, "has blue skin because he's absorbed all the poisons of the mind for all beings in the world and vowed to assist all those suffering or sick." She explained that Amchi was going to offer us a taste of the power and wisdom of this Buddha so that all of us could benefit from his healing wisdom.

I could certainly use some of this wisdom healing, *I thought. Joan's words from last night right before dinner lingered in my mind: "The Dalai Lama says that compassion is his religion." I recalled how the first Dalai Lama was appointed by a Mongolian shaman ruler named Altan Khan 500 years ago. This is where our traditions meet, I said to myself.*

Less is more. Joan knows that, and it is what makes her such an excellent teacher. After her brief introduction, Amchi began with an invocation and then came to each of us and sprinkled water from a copper jar on our heads before stroking our foreheads with a peacock feather fan.

I felt absolutely nothing, no shift into an altered state of being. Then, as I noticed how nice it was to feel nothing, the chatter inside my head stopped. Empty yet joyful. The critic was silent. The anthropologist in me who was always observing and taking notes instead of being fully present and engaging life was taking a nap.

What a relief. All along, the poison was my own mind, end-less thinking to avoid simply being.

Please, Medicine Buddha, make my mind shut up for once, *I thought.* Let me know stillness.

And then, I did. There was nothing, no ripple on the water. Only the quiet.

Hummingbird medicine is the next gift on the wisdom wheel. It gives you the power to become the solution instead of looking for the solution and racking your brain to figure out how to make it manifest. Hummingbird's gift is that it teaches you to recognize that you are the problem that needs addressing. If you take yourself and your need to dominate out of the equation, you allow order, healing, and harmony to emerge spontaneously. Yet as with all the directions on the wheel, hummingbird offers you a challenge: to let go of the need to heal yourself so you can heal so much more than the personal pain of one person on the planet.

The Lessons of Hummingbird

When we have the gift of hummingbird wisdom, we spare ourselves much suffering because we know when to speak and when to be silent, when to act and when to simply observe. We stop getting in our own way as we reclaim our birthright as co-creators of beauty and harmony and as sages drawing upon wisdom beyond our own. We redefine what our "work" is: we stop mistaking our career or job for what we are here to do. All of us are here to be, to learn, to teach, to heal, to inspire, and so on, and this work can take many forms, changing over time.

As we learn to be still like a hummingbird in flight and witness what we are experiencing, reorganizing the outer world will happen naturally without our having to exert extra effort. And when we do act, we are more likely to be in alignment with our purpose rather than acting from a need to fix the world around us and get it to conform to our expectations.

In Greek mythology, the male energy of the sun, represented by Helios, drove a golden chariot across the sky from the East in the morning, reaching the West at evening. Though worship of the patriarchal Greek gods fell out of favor in ancient times, the emphasis on action continues to influence Western thought and philosophy. When faced with a dilemma, we tend to launch into a plan of attack. We make actionable goals. But there are alternatives: We could consider multiple approaches to co-creating a solution, be open to receiving input from Spirit as well as others willing to work with us, and engage in a more nuanced process of collaboration. We could choose to still our actions and mind and be receptive to the wisdom of the invisible realm, which would offer us the potential for a big "Aha!" that takes us forward into a new way of being. The humble hummingbird reminds us that our way of living has become imbalanced, too focused on everyday concerns and our personal needs and longings. We have much to learn from this tiny creature.

Hummingbirds measure just a few inches across, yet annually they migrate all the way from Canada to South America, stopping to refuel only after flying countless miles over the ocean, when they reach Cuba. They embark on this journey regardless of the odds against them. And wherever they feed, drawing in the nectar of flowers through their long beaks, they leave behind traces of pollen from other blossoms. This exchange demonstrates reciprocity: they receive life-sustaining nourishment and contribute to the flowers by pollinating them. They don't gather any more nectar than is necessary.

The gift of hummingbird medicine is to see our lives as mythic journeys like the ones countless others have taken and will take, grand journeys in which the names and details change. We may not know the names and faces of our ancestors who overcame hardship, traveling far from their homes over lands and seas that were often inhospitable, risking all to follow a dream of a better life or the call to exploration. We may never know the stories of individuals who fought to protect their clans or villages and preserve their way of life in the face of those who hoped to wipe them out and take over their grounds for hunting and gathering. But we recognize ourselves and the possibilities for us that are inherent in the inspiring lore passed down through oral traditions (and more recently, in books and movies).

Sometimes we will engage in fantasies of standing out from the crowd, of leading the charge. That happens when it doesn't feel like enough to be just another brave sojourner when we could be the one about whom great songs will be written and stories will be told long after our demise. Understandably, we crave accolades and success. In Western culture, the emphasis on individual achievement has caused many of us to struggle with the idea that we can be important without being the one on the top of the hierarchy of power and influence. We want to be the all-important "king of the hill." Hummingbird medicine allows us to see that small acts that may go mostly unnoticed can have powerful reverberations. Small nonactions, moments in which one person simply witnesses what is, remaining still and radiating peace, are powerful. Making a big difference in the world through some extraordinary act isn't the goal; it's a natural outcome, and it involves more people than just you or me.

The desire to be acknowledged for our individual achievements is driven by the patriarchal drive: we've forgotten what an extraordinary honor and thrill it is to play even a very small, destined-to-be-forgotten role in the larger story of the human experience. In contrast, when we're in touch with our matriarchal instinct, we recognize the value of our individual contribution in harmony with that of others and of the times. We see that life isn't a competition focused on victory but on collaborative interaction. We take action and sit quietly, witnessing all that arises in the silence and stillness. We step forth and back, knowing when to give and when to receive, carrying out a harmonious and exquisite dance.

In our quest to heal ourselves—and the Earth—the most important action for us to take might be simply to quiet our restless minds. When we become still, like the humming-bird who appears motionless in flight, a great witness within us is awakened and arises. At last, we recognize the story we are caught up in and simply observe it, breathing into it, in the quiet space of our heart, not judging ourselves or the people who contributed to our suffering—or even the suf-fering of the Earth and her creatures. All of us came to this life to do the work of co-creation. In stillness, we become not just healers but sages, clear on when to act and when to simply witness what is happening. This is quite different from doing nothing because we remain present and deeply restful yet ready to take action if needed.

In the North, the direction of the hummingbird, we can enter into the mythic Eden, the fabled paradise from which we were ejected, where we can eat from the tree of knowl-edge of good and evil without any fear of punishment. Here is the garden where sages can grow their wisdom. In this lush and fertile land, we can once again recognize who we are in our fullness and know what it is to be our natural selves. We once again walk in beauty, speak to the rivers and trees and clouds, and dialogue with Spirit, just as we did when in our original paradisial state. We discover we can have a reciprocal, collaborative relationship with the divine. Then, we choose to live in ayni, in harmony.

Ayni and Saying Yes to Possibility

We're challenged to interact with others and the world around us as the hummingbird gives and takes in relationship to a flower: Seek harmony. Help the Earth as she helps you. Contribute to the well-being of the planet and to others without needing to have a newspaper story written about you. Don't give in to the fear that scarcity and disaster will result if you don't stuff your face, your basement, or your head right now. Trust in the wisdom and nourishment that is available to you on your journey in this lifetime. Say yes to possibility by letting go of your patriarchal instinct to define exactly what that possibility is. Open to the mystical experience of co-creation.

Mastering ayni, living in harmony with heaven, Earth, and the quantum field of possibility, frees you from a scarcity mind-set. It makes you realize that the more you give to others, the more abundance and beauty come your way. You will receive the nectar you need. Pachamama always provides—but we tend to forget that.

In the creation myth of the Mapuche people of Central Chile with whom my wife, Marcela, trained, the first divine being was female and gave birth to a jaguar that ended up growling at her mother and running off into the wild. The second child of this deity was a cougar that nursed from the mother's breast. The third child was human and proceeded to populate the Earth. This myth tells us that the first beings created were the wild creatures, who have the privilege of the firstborn. The second, represented by the cougar, were the creatures who have a relationship with humans and whom we would domesticate. The humans are in third place. The takeaway is twofold: The first lesson is that as we go off into the world, we have to honor our mother and not forget to return to her for nourishment, for she will always support us. The second lesson is that we must protect all that is wild. We receive from nature but give to it too, fostering its well-being, living in ayni. This is what Mother Earth wants from us.

Living in ayni means a joyful surrender to the process in which you are a participant, a co-creator with the quantum field. The field seeks to bring order out of chaos and offers you the wisdom and assistance to create a new vision for humanity. Living in ayni means being willing to admit when you're wrong but also standing up when you feel strongly that you're right—that what you have to contribute has value. Your demonstrating to others that you are open to learning, to collaborating and creating, to healing and listening, changes the field, sending out reverberations that will motivate others. And these others might do even more than you do to bring about a better world for all to inhabit.

All of us must undertake this work of the hummingbird for the good of Mother Earth and all life. We must master right relationship, thinking, and action, rather than looking for Pachamama to rescue us or assuming we have to take the reins so we can be sure our own interests are served first.

Mother Earth and Us

Of course, we want to survive and thrive as individuals, but our focus needs to shift now to the Earth, which we have badly mistreated. It is undergoing trials of earth, water, wind, and fire. We're seeing the soil depleted of nutrients and toxified by pesticides and man-made chemicals that foul our water. Hurricanes, drought, and flooding all reveal disturbances in the planet's water cycle. Hurricanes are a symptom of disturbed wind. The wind carries toxins from factories into the lungs of people and animals. Plants that can naturally cleanse the air can't keep up with the amount of pollution we're producing. Massive wildfires are destroying forests because we haven't been responsible stewards of the land, and we resist the inconvenience of allowing controlled burns to prevent more devastating fires. You can do all the healing work on yourself that you want and try to bring beauty, peace, and harmony to your family only to be driven out of your home and your familiar lifestyle by disasters caused by our disrespect for Mother Earth.

Pachamama recognizes humans as parasitic infections that have to be controlled—or eliminated. We are supposed to be stewards of the health of the natural world, which provides us with beneficial microbes that live in our gut, and sunlight that allows our bodies to produce vitamin D and contributes to our health and well-being. Unfortunately, we have not lived up to our obligations. To save the Earth, we have to heal ourselves. And to heal ourselves, we have to save the Earth. This is the nature of our interconnectedness, or ayni, with Pachamama.

Every one of us is made of Earth and Spirit and is part of the quantum field. As you learned earlier, each of us has a personal energy field woven into the quantum field of the cosmos. We need to embody the wisdom that can guide us to the work we came here to do: contributing to the well-being of all. Hummingbird medicine can nurture us with the pure nectar of life and make us think twice about becoming distracted by needless hectic activity. We need to engage in the highest form of ayni to help birth a new relationship with the Earth and with each other.

It's difficult to resist the temptation to play the hero who dashes in to salvage a situation or rescue someone, sure that we know what has to be done. But we don't want to blunder about, blinded by our need to feel important and by our distorted preconceived notions. We have to stop, become still, observe, and let wisdom arise naturally within us. That's easier to do when we are meditating or in nature. However, too many of us are out of balance with our own bodies. Our natural instincts have gone awry because our fight-or-flight system is turned up to full volume: we sleep yet do not rest; we sit in meditation, yet our minds can't seem to stop chasing thoughts. But if we enter silence and find the witness within us, the hand of Spirit can operate silently and bring order out of chaos. As I said before, witnessing, which is one gift of hummingbird medicine, does not mean not doing anything. It means allowing things to happen organically, allowing beauty to emerge out of chaos naturally and spontaneously, as it does when you are in ayni and your mind is still. I am not talking about mindlessly channel surfing or scrolling through your social media feed. While meditation, stillness, and watching a football game or the latest cat video may all look similar, they are vastly different. In meditation and stillness, you disappear. You lose all personal importance. You say to Spirit, "For I have ceased to exist, only you are here." Zoning out to relax is all about you and your desires. The world and the galaxies spin around your banal sense of self-importance and your need for comfort and entertainment.

While you might protest that this is not the case, the truth is that the couch is very seductive, and the big change you might say you want is quite different from the one you need. The transformation you seek is not going to be other people and situations altering themselves to meet your needs or your ideas about how things "should" be. It's going to be your own transformation.

Avoiding the Seduction of Returning to Old Ways

In the journey through the wisdom wheel, we gather personal power if we can manage to avoid being seduced by greed, glory, and the promise of instant gratification. Saying yes to Spirit's call to us means that we must be willing to make uncomfortable changes. We must prioritize the well-being of the planet and, after that, its creatures. Only then do we prioritize people—including those in our own communities. All the therapy and detoxing we do won't matter if we, like everyone else, have no safe place to hide from the planet's upheavals. We are going to have to let go of some old ways. On some level, we know this, but the yearning to "get back to normal" is strong. The familiarity of how we used to operate is seductive. But as I said earlier, we need to move forward, evolving as a species and creating a new way of being.

While helping people and fixing situations might seem like the next step after shedding all that was holding you back from experiencing, even briefly, your spiritual and eternal nature, that's not what's needed. The skills you have built to help yourself, others, and Mother Earth and her creatures will be valuable. But you will have to set them aside long enough to see how they may have become tainted by a need to be seen as important and special and by a desire to fix situations that cause you distress. You have to become still, observe the naked truth of what you're doing and why, and witness that you are not alone and unsupported in your desire to help the Earth, humanity, and yourself thrive.

Remember, your wisdom pales in comparison to the wisdom in the invisible world where you can connect with the lineage of the wisdom teachers—the Alto Mesayok that the shamans of the Andes speak of and which the Buddhists call the bodhisattvas. They are the ones from the past and the future who have mastered timelessness and are helping us create a world our children can be born into. Ancient lore says that Pachacuti was the last great Inca and that he stepped outside of time; that is, he became an enlightened Buddha-like being who no longer needed to heal past wounds from his many incarnations on Earth. In the East, they would say he had freed himself of karma. (*Pacha* means "earth" or "time," and *kuti* means "to step outside of" or "to turn over.") It's said that Pachacuti predicted the turning point we are at now, a moment when we must choose a destiny that will lead to our evolution rather than our extinction. We are in the time of the great turning over of the Earth, challenged to follow Pachacuti in his footsteps. The more of us who choose to accept a destiny of evolution, who agree to walk the road less traveled, which can take us into a more desirable future, the better chance humanity has to survive and even thrive.

Hummingbird medicine will bring us gently to this destiny.

Accepting That Endings Have to Occur

Ayni with our time means recognizing the inevitability of change, meaning we have to be willing to let things come to an end. In Hinduism, the divine has three aspects: the destroyer, the creator, and the maintainer. The destructive aspect of the divine isn't woven into the religions in the West, even though we know that in the natural world species are born, thrive, and die. Some life-forms die to make room for new ones that fill the ecological niche the others vacated. And floods and forest fires are necessary for clearing the woods and offering an opportunity for new life to emerge. Right now, there is much about the "old normal" that we will have to leave behind—yet we're lethargic and resisting change.

We like to think of the mother energy as all-nurturing and loving and ignore her fierce and destructive side. We do have a myth about rising like a phoenix from the flames, which captures this idea that out of disaster and destruction comes renewal, new life. And we have the story of Jesus rising from the dead just as new life rises after the dead of winter. But too often, we forget that destruction and endings need to exist. We have to learn to accept the reality that for things to be born, other things must die. Rather than allowing our species to become extinct, we must let some things die— including our selfish and unsustainable ways of using the Earth's resources.

The Menominee Nation in what is now Wisconsin has a long history of practicing healthy forestry, and now people of European descent are coming to them to learn from them. The Menominee make sure there is a diversity of growth within the woods—trees both old and young—as well as a variety of plants to maintain balance and prevent out-of-control burning. They have inventoried 58,000 trees—more than 30 species—and keep track of their height and diameter, managing the forest carefully to be sure it remains viable for future generations.[1] While lightning strikes can set off a fire just as a human can, respectful attention paid to our forests and the rest of the natural world can prevent unnecessary levels of destruction. This is what ayni with nature looks like: love, protection, and respectful stewardship, balancing endings and beginnings, death and life. Ayni means recognizing there are limits to the comforts we can enjoy without overburdening Mother Earth, who sometimes needs her forests to burn, her shorelines to go underwater, and her waters to flood the land. When we understand and respect that, we open to more radical ideas regarding our relationship to our planet.

Practice Ayni with the Ancestors

Just as we practice ayni with nature, we must practice ayni with the ancestors. I'm not talking about honoring the elders in your community or your literal grandparents, although that is important. I'm referring to a practice of tapping into the wisdom of the sages of old whose teachings have become lost or forgotten. You accomplish this by releasing your identification with your name and your body to access the guidance available beyond the gate.

In the past, wisdom keepers around the globe were often persecuted and even tortured, their writings destroyed, their oral traditions ridiculed. However, you can still receive their guidance if you set and hold on to the intention of opening to the timeless stillness of the witness. Then you can bring this wisdom latent in the quantum field into your personal energy field and out into your community. You offer ayni—respect and love—to the ancestors, who in turn offer you the gift of becoming a sage.

When you hear the voices of the ancients, when you see the visions they provide you when you have shifted out of ordinary perception and left behind its distractions, you will recognize that the sages of old do not need you to repeat exactly what they have spoken. Instead, you can find your own voice, your own mission, your own calling and songs. This must be done from a place of deep humility, however. Beware of your arrogance getting in your way.

At the Four Winds Society, we had a student, a young man who was a graduate of our training, who was a quick study. Everything he learned in class seemed second nature, as if he had been nursed on the milk of the ancient shamanic wisdom. One day after class, he came to me and explained that he realized that he was a reincarnation of Pachacuti.

"Great," I said. "This means you have much work to do to help usher in the new era for humanity."

I had just spoken that day about how Pachacuti is an archetype, what the ancients would call a deity—and which today we understand as a universal quality. You can become Pachacuti-like and help bring in an age of peace to the planet in the same way that you can become Buddha-like. But I did not realize that this young man believed he was actually the reincarnation of the Inca emperor, builder of Machu Picchu and the greatest empire the world had known since Genghis Khan.

A few days later, I received a call from Don Manuel, who was in Cusco.

"One of your students is here," he said. "He claims he is the Pachacuti, and he traveled to Hatun Q'ero to bring a message to our people."

I could feel my stomach starting to turn. Hatun Q'ero is the village of the last of the Inca shamans, located at an altitude of 4,000 meters. It is a three-day walk from the nearest road—that is, if you don't get caught in a snowstorm along the way, which can happen even in the summer.

"He asked me for a shamanic name," Don Manuel continued, "so I gave him the name Wayra Uma, the condor that flies high."

I couldn't help but start laughing. The literal translation of Wayra Uma from the Quechua language is "airhead."

The old man went on. "Word had reached the village before he arrived, and they welcomed him as the Son of the Sun."

The Inca lore says that the Inca Pachacuti will return someday to free his people from the bondage of the conquistadors. He will have great shamanic powers, including the ability to heal the sick, call the rain, and summon the thunder and the lightning. And he might come from any race or culture in the world, not necessarily from the Andes, so to the people of the village, the notion of a blond Pachacuti was not too far-fetched.

Don Manuel went on to explain that the young man had announced himself as their king. It was midsummer in the Andes, and there would be no rain or lighting for many months until the first rains arrived in the fall, so the villagers asked my student to summon the lightning. Unaware that he would be required to prove his claim, he turned around and began hiking back to the city, leaving much laughter in his wake.

The young man returned to our classes later that year heartbroken. Men can be easily seduced by a sense of self-importance just as they are easily seduced by a woman or sexy idea. My student learned a big lesson. And the incident started the legend of the blond Pachacuti that everyone is still chuckling about to this day.

New Myths

Myths, rituals, and interpretations of wisdom teachings change over time, just as the forest, ocean, and desert do. This is why the shamans readily embrace a new expression of an ancient myth or archetype. In contrast, people who practice religion often are intent on holding on to the old form—for example, only the ancient Sanskrit or Hebrew of sacred texts. The letters become magical: religious leaders realize the words contain power and hold secrets that must be carefully guarded. Form takes precedence over substance.

The sacred maps and language shift as we develop wisdom. The Founding Fathers of the United States put forth the vision that "all men are created equal," but it took well over a century for that vision to include more than male landowners of European descent. It took time for stories in the Bible to be interpreted in ways that didn't involve burning medicine women at the stake (allowing a "witch" to live is forbidden in the Old Testament). We honor those who came before, who wrote the stories and devised the rituals, by bringing ancient voices alive and making their messages contemporary.

Hummingbird wisdom lets you remember stories you have never heard before, to voice a wisdom that flows through you but that you did not acquire directly. This greater wisdom offers new possibilities instead of harmful and antiquated ideas such as "Let's have these people be in power over all those others, who are greater in number, and serve the superior ones at the top of the heap." Or "Women are here to serve men, bearing their babies and being their helpmates, with only the occasional woman accomplishing something of importance because she cannot find a man or give birth to a son." We have a lot of old ideas that need to go onto the compost pile. In becoming still and becoming the witness, you can cease seeking wisdom in books and philosophies. You can become wise beyond your years and experiences, but only if you are still long enough to cross the gateway to stillness. And you can only achieve genuine still-ness after you have acquired jaguar and serpent medicine that have healed you and prepared you for this crossing.

In practicing ayni with the ancient sages, you can access wisdom on the other side of the rainbow bridge and see with new eyes. You can pick up on nuances and see grays instead of just black-and-white. Your old binary way of perceiving—of this versus that, us versus them, male versus female, good versus evil—gives way to a more sophisticated way of understanding the interactions among people and energies. You cease looking for "the truth" and begin to bring meaning, healing, and harmony into whatever situation you find yourself in. You will be too busy creating truth and bringing meaning to every situation to look for "the truth" or "the way" to enlightenment anymore. There is an old saying: the way of hummingbird medicine cannot be found by seeking, but only those who seek may find it.

And you can create a new myth for yourself. You may find your job changing, even disappearing completely, leaving you with a sense that you have lost your identity. But remember: You are on a mythic journey. Your work in this lifetime will take many forms. You can transform who you are, finding purpose in endeavors you hadn't even thought about before change was thrust upon you.

When you live in ayni, you stop trying so hard to control and determine your personal future and instead learn and receive the wisdom of the ancients. Then your work becomes clear to you. To do this work, however, you must master time and invisibility.

Mastering Time

In Western culture, we are taught that time is linear, like an arrow that takes us from the past into the present and then on to the future. Causes are in the past, effects are felt now or at a later time, and we are trapped by fate: the fate of statistics, of tragedy in love, of mistaking our job for our work, of subscribing to beliefs that contradict our spiritual wisdom and nature. Shamans understand that this linear time is only one of several kinds of time; time can also be circular, like a turning wheel or spiral. What we are experiencing now might have been caused by something yet to happen that is reaching back through the spiral of sacred time to influence us today. A multitude of destinies and possibilities can arise out of the seeming disorder of past, present, and future mingling together in the complex, multidimensional realm beyond the rainbow bridge.

The problem with linear time is that it ends. As the sages of old set about trying to solve the problem of disease and old age, they realized that they had to solve the problem of linear time: it is haunted by death and ruled by fate, which preordains you to live and suffer and die the way that your ancestors did. The past determines the future. The ancients realized they needed to learn to work with nonlinear time, and they did it by expanding causality to include synchronicity and observing the interconnectedness of past, present, and future in the middle world of everyday reality and in the present moment.

In polychronic, sacred time, which is accessible in the invisible world, you can experience past, present, and future concurrently. You can break out of the limitations of cause and effect. You can taste infinity and navigate the rivers of time that allow you to travel into the past, ride the tides that flow into the future, and explore—and then escape—the eddies that keep us stuck in the moment.

The shaman employs the skill of mastering time to discover who we will become 10,000 years from today and then bring that wisdom from the future back to now. This is how the prophets of old foretold the terrible mess that we find ourselves in. They saw the destiny lines of humanity converging in a point of crisis and cataclysm—climate collapse, species extinction, disease. And they foresaw a new humanity emerging after this pivotal event that they called the pachakuti, the singularity at the end of time, of an era—named after the Inca leader who mastered timelessness. They realized we could become a new human that could grow a new body infused with wisdom and health, one that would age, heal, live, and die differently—and perhaps never die.

Or we could become extinct.

The future isn't predetermined. But your life is. You can choose a different destiny or stumble your way into a nicer fate than the one that seems to be at the end of the road you are on. But if you want to consciously choose the destiny of evolving into a new human, *homo luminous*, and firmly place yourself on that trajectory instead of the one you've been cast on, you have to do more than wish and hope things get better. You must learn to be still and to observe synchronicities. These are signs that remind us that linear time is only a pervasive illusion, one that feels very real in the everyday world but that dissipates when we enter the invisible realm, much like it does when we are sleeping and enter our dreams. You must allow yourself to become a witness, fully present in the timeless moment without needing to steer it this way or that, so that the sacred—sacred love, sacred wisdom—can make itself known within you.

If you have the courage to do that, you will start to remember that you are here to co-create a new dream with the divine and make it manifest. Then, you will remember that when plans go awry, it's not that the universe is conspiring against you, but rather that it's prodding you along to discard a narrow, limited fate and step into a greater destiny.

It wants all of us to do the sacred work we came here to do.

It can be hard to accept that maybe you aren't meant to hold onto that job you loved but lost, or to remain in a relationship with someone you loved deeply but who couldn't be in a reciprocal and loving union with you. By mastering timelessness, you learn that the universe is always pushing you to experience a journey you mapped out with Spirit before you came here, a destiny that involves loss, learning, and love in a dance whose beauty and complexity you see better in hindsight.

Slowing Down When Life Is Speeding Up

Mastering time, stepping into your experience of the sacred, involves a shift in perspective that is very difficult to bring about when you're constantly in motion, speeding through life while trying to manage all that is thrown at you. You must learn to do nothing, practicing patience regardless of the seduction of the clock that challenges you to race it.

Fear of death, which we worked to release in the West, keeps us running at a mad pace to get everything done before our time is up. It keeps us seduced by the belief that if we stay busy enough, death will simply have to wait for our all-important tasks to be done. With hummingbird medicine, we stop the clock as we practice stillness in the midst of all the activity, witnessing without acting, just as the hummingbird practices stillness in flight. We notice the space between breaths and heartbeats. Our stillness dissolves the seductive distractions that keep us on the move and exhausting ourselves as we operate as human doings rather than human beings.

I found this body of teaching very confusing at the beginning. After all, I thought of myself as a man of action. I hated to waste time—even sleeping—because life is full of things to do. Later, I realized that I had spent decades running at a hundred miles an hour and getting nowhere. I remembered a conversation I had with Don Manuel, where he told me I had to learn to breathe. "Breathe like a baby," he once said to me. "Not like a dog, panting."

Most people normally take 10 to 14 breaths every minute. This is the sign of an overtaxed and stressed system. I had to learn to slow my breathing, to take only four to five breaths a minute, holding my breath empty for a moment at the bottom of the breath and full for a moment at the top. I soon discovered that as I breathed gently and slowly, my world slowed down and I accomplished much more while doing much less running around.

Becoming still and patient allows us to see that not every problem has to be addressed right away. We can remain present with whatever is going on as we access wisdom and love and allow healing to begin without our having to run around looking for a bandage or a balm, the perfect words to say, or the right advice to offer. We can stop doing and simply be—witnessing what is happening as one moment gives way to another. This is difficult when we can simply use our phones to research something on the Internet or to find a distracting photo or news item to dive into. Stillness means being patient so that you can connect with the invisible realm of magic and mystery, poised between the past and the future in the absolute present, with no remorse for what has been, no dreams that will turn into nightmares.

Don Manuel also taught the practice of "letting it be": whatever challenge or difficulty he faced, he simply allowed it to be and unfold on its own, infusing it only with an intention to help bring about the highest good for all. He and my original mentor, Don Antonio, believed that even the Conquest and the devastation of the great Andean civilization was for some greater good that they could not yet comprehend. They mourned what they perceived as "the great evil from Europe," yet did not try to correct it. They only shared the truth as they understood it: the truth about our stewardship of Mother Earth, about being grateful for the sunrise that day, about helping the sick. This was ayni with the times. Don Manuel once said that we begin our practice of ayni to please our teachers, and then we make ayni out of habit, and finally, we practice ayni because we feel in our hearts the yearning for tasting divine wisdom in timelessness. Then, we find the time for spiritual practice, because life itself is a spiritual practice.

Toward the end of our lives, or after a close brush with death, we become more aware of our mortality and more likely to focus on what we most want to do, yet we also discover the power of a moment in which we do nothing. No chores get done, no blank spots in our education get filled in, and no stories get told and reexamined. Instead of becoming stuck in analysis paralysis, we put a halt to the ruminating. The complaining and worrying and planning we did in the past now seems like a colossal waste of time.

Hummingbird medicine helps you develop the skill of doing things at the right time, not according to a schedule. It gives you the ability to operate in sacred time, going back to events that happened in the past and changing your relationship to them: how you hold them in your memories and in your energy field, and how they affect you in your day-to-day life. You learn the lessons and release the resentment, anger, fear, and grief.

When you master timelessness, you create space in your life—or rather, it creates itself. You have time for what matters. You don't kid yourself that this reality of the senses is the only one, that anything you've ever experienced in the invisible realm wasn't real—that it was simply an illusion and a pleasant one but not of any importance. You have a new relationship to this notion of "reality" in the "real world."

Reality Is a Relative Thing

One of our fears about time running out is that we—that the essence of who we are, and all our memories—will cease to exist at the moment of death. Amazon shamans, on the other hand, believe you get nine lives (more or less), like jaguars and cats do, to attain infinity. If you can't master timelessness by then, you get composted, so to say: Your memories and consciousness become absorbed into the black hole of death and don't retain their integrity. You missed your chance. They point out how rare and precious it is to acquire a human body, how our life must not be wasted, our opportunities lost.

To attain infinity, to continue to exist beyond death, it helps to have a mission bigger than me, than Alberto. It requires letting go of the belief that what you see, feel, think, do, and plan is of the highest value. You have to stop being in love with your own importance and instead become still and know that you are intrinsically intertwined with the cosmos. You always have been. You always will be. That becomes clear when you become still and witness that inseparable relationship.

Quiet the mind and you see the true nature of reality reflected everywhere, like the surface of a still lake. The slightest breeze and the ripples reflect only the surface of the lake; the reflection of the trees and the sky become turbulent and distorted. You see only relative truth, not absolute truth. You perceive relative reality but not absolute impermanent reality. Reality is evanescent. And it's determined by your perception. What's more, your perception and mine can be different in any given moment. If you and I agree on a subjective reality, we should enjoy that moment because it will be fleeting thanks to the eternally changing nature of life. When you learn to be still and open your heart to the mystery and the complexity of the human experience, you do not make such a big deal about what your relative reality is right now. The nuances become clear, and you find it easier to give up the black-and-white, binary thinking that offers a comforting—if deluded—sense of control in an uncertain world.

The challenge is to stop worrying about your relative reality and trying to hammer it into a shape that pleases you. Even if you succeed, your reality will morph again. It's not easy to stop focusing only on curing a disease or illness you're suffering from and instead focus on transforming it into a turning point on your life journey. It's hard to stop thinking about changing your job and finding a similar position elsewhere when you are being called to find your true work, what you came here to do in this lifetime. You might reject the idea that instead of replacing your romantic partner, you should transform the relationship you have now—and do this by transforming yourself, by becoming the partner you would want to have. In short, the lesson of hummingbird medicine is to stop trying to treat symptoms and instead address underlying causes. You're asked to claim and effectively use the power that is available to you when you disidentify with who you believe you are. You join in the grand work of dreaming with the sages, shaping the sacred dream that will morph into being if enough of us dream it together.

The truth is that bad things will happen to you no matter how hard you try to remain safe and avoid suffering. You can be meticulous about caring for your health, excel at your work, and be completely devoted to having the strongest marriage possible, and it can all hit the fan for reasons that may have nothing to do with your choices or actions. You are only one person co-creating reality. Eight billion other people are doing the same thing. And a lot of them are contributing to a nightmare rather than a brilliant dream that will allow you and humanity to thrive.

But there is good news. You can, if only for a brief time, experience absolute reality. This is where all possibilities converge. It's where your worries, resentments, and regrets dissolve as you experience the perfection of a moment. There is pain, and there is also beauty. The gift of hummingbird is the love that you can experience when you stop rushing about trying to change your life and choose instead to witness the wheel of fortune as it continues to turn. In stillness is peace and the hope that you might get a glimpse of your destiny, of the impact you can make if you stop struggling to make an impact.

Mastering Invisibility

The shaman summons the power, knowledge, and love that exist in the invisible realms outside of time. These inform her energy field. Her identity shifts as she recognizes that she has had many incarnations: she has inhabited many bodies that have experienced both pleasure and pain. She knows that "I" is beyond the limitations of the body—of gender, age, ethnicity, and so on. She is able to be the caretaker of the future rather than the custodian of the past who is stuck keeping the old dream going when it has already turned into a nightmare. The old "I" who had all of these labels attached to it dissolves as the shaman surrenders her identity.

To accomplish this, you must allow the limited sense of self to die, and learn to disappear.

While you, the self you know, inhabits and is fixed to a body, "you" are actually a being of conscious energy within the larger quantum field. And you, that bit of energy, are influenced by fluctuations in the field. Physics explains that the electron can be either a particle or a wave. In fact, when you are looking for the electron, the wave function collapses and the particle appears where you are looking for it. The German physicist Werner Heisenberg discovered this and called it the uncertainty principle (also known as the experimenter effect). Because of this phenomenon, we interact with and influence everything we are near and direct our attention toward, even if we don't realize it's happening. Reality is influenced by what you expect it to be, and your expectations are shaped by your history as well as your ideas about who you are and what you can accomplish.

The shaman's challenge to become invisible is based on the same notion that we influence everything we observe. Even our mere presence and the energy we radiate disturbs or balances the field. The quality of your vibes affects and twists reality. You can choose to stop sending the certainty of your convictions about the world and what your life is or should be like, about who you are and what you can and should do, into the field. What you put out is what you will find mirrored back to you. The electron, like Dr. Heisenberg pointed out, will always be where you look for it.

If you've ever spent time around someone who is relentlessly pessimistic, you know what it's like to feel your vitality slipping away as they carry on about how awful the weather is, how impossible their situations are, how troubled the world is, and how much worse things are getting each day. The universe will always prove biases and prejudices right. It will draw people and situations who match your beliefs about the world to you, even as you're drawn to them. Opportunities to prove that you were right, that life's a bitch after all, will show up for you as evidence that other people can't be trusted and that the world is going to hell.

When you understand this, you can recognize that together, we are dreaming the world into being. Every thought, every wish, every bit of anger or love we as individuals send out organizes our experience of the world. Too many people are sending out the message that we all might as well give up and self-medicate until reality changes because there's no hope of our changing it. They put forth an impressive effort to convince the rest of us that they are justified in their cynicism and pessimism, and the world reflects back to them that yes, they are right.

You are invited to become still and accept that life is both wondrous and monstrous. When you do that, it becomes easier to let go of your need to ensure that you use your willpower to burn out your friend's melancholic mood, your in-laws' negative attitudes and prejudices, and all the ugliness, suffering, and cruelty in the world. All of that will be out there. You don't have to clean it all up by yourself, and if you think that's your job, you're going to miss out on your chances to experience wisdom that helps you know just what to do or not do when you encounter the hideousness. Here's the paradox: once you're invisible, freed from the need to impose your will on a situation, your power to affect it increases exponentially.

At a practical level, recognize that you can change anything if you let someone else take credit for it. Let go of your need to play a particular role in the process of change, in the movement that includes many more people than just you and your friends. You become your own worst obstacle when you are sure what the right way to do things is, when you are more interested in being right than in doing right.

If you master invisibility, it doesn't mean that others will not see you or that they won't acknowledge your contribution. It means that you cease to be at the center of your life and renounce the need to be in the spotlight. You become more concerned with *we* than *me*.

Master invisibility by abstaining from saying or thinking, "I want" and "I need." Try it for an entire hour. Then try it for an entire day. You can go ahead and eat meals, stretch, do your work, parent your kids—but do it without wanting and needing, without telling yourself that your life isn't good enough, that the people you love are inadequate and so are you, that something has to change or be fixed.

When you master invisibility, you discover that the underlying reality of the cosmos isn't data or information, as science might have us think, but wisdom.

The shaman who has shed the stories of the past, the need to be important, the fears around not being seen or sufficiently loved, can learn directly from the sages of the past. She can gain wisdom without needing a teacher. Rather than being the wise fool who knows a little and thinks she is an expert, she has opened to wisdom beyond what any one person can develop in a lifetime.

The challenge of the hummingbird, like that of the other directions, requires dedication to achieving mastery through practice. Reconnect with nature, meditate, and use the exercises in this book, including the fire ceremonies, doing them daily if you can. That way, you will become closer to mastering ayni with nature and the ancestors, tasting infinity and disappearing, all of which will allow you to dream a new sacred dream.

To do the fire ceremony for hummingbird, rather than gather a pile of sticks to create death arrows and life arrows, use an herb bundle (lavender, sage, rosemary, or other dried herbs tied together). You'll touch this to the fire to burn away comforts and cleanse any imprints these seductions have made on your energy body. Instead of using your hands to draw the transformative power of the fire into your energy body, you'll touch the bundle to the candle flame to infuse it with new energies to be installed. You'll again work within sacred space and do a conversation with your power animal, but with this ceremony—and with the fire ceremony for eagle—make a point of being fully present in the moment of the void or emptiness before you bring into your field the energy you want to install in it. It's important to allow yourself to feel this emptiness. Resist the temptation to bring in the energy you think you need. Your ideas might be more limited than you realize, so you're going to be burning them away and simply bringing in transformative energy that will help awaken your natural instincts and allow deep wisdom to arise within you.

Fire Ceremony for Hummingbird

Prepare for the ceremony as instructed, open sacred space, and when you are ready, with the fire lit, your notebook and pen beside you, your bundle of herbs in hand, identify any creature comforts you have become convinced you can't live without. Name them. Then, touch the bundle to the candle flame to release the energies connected to these attachments. When you have done so, pause in stillness. Witness your mood, your state of being.

Now bring the smoking bundle to your energy field near your lower three chakras to cleanse them with fire and smoke. Pause, witnessing what you are experiencing. Then, touch the bundle to the fire again to bring its transformative energies into the bundle that you will use to transfer them into your lower three chakras.

Next, you will give up your psychological comforts: your belief that you're a likable, good person, that you have the strength to handle all the challenges you'll face, that you are important and making a difference in the world. If there was a life path that has helped you to feel accepted and secure, whether it was one that seems to have been preselected for you or that you pursued despite any pressures from people around you to make different choices, let it go as you touch the bundle to the fire again, burning away this life path. Pause in silence, feeling the emptiness. Then, use the smoking bundle to cleanse your heart, throat, and forehead chakras. Be still. Be present. Be.

Now touch the bundle to the fire again and bring the energy of the fire, of Mother Earth, of the possibility of new love and new feelings, to your energy field. Install it in your heart, throat, and forehead chakras.

Next, give up your comforting ideas about God and goodness, the stories about how everything will turn out right in the end if you just stay true to your innate goodness and do your best. Release any ideologies and concepts that have trapped you, anything you feel you need to advocate for or be an activist for, anything that makes you feel an urgent need to do, fix, or resolve something. And release any grand notions about what you need to do before you die. Do this by touching the bundle to the fire, which will burn them away and transform them. Pause. Be still.

Then use the smoking bundle to cleanse your entire field, from your toes all the way up to your crown, or seventh, chakra above your head. After doing this, remain still in the silence so that you can experience the void, observing but not judging, not interpreting, not planning or hoping but simply being present in the experience.

Now touch the bundle to the fire to bring in the wisdom of the ancient sages and the great maps of destiny that have been lost or that have yet to be drawn, the ideas that have yet to be explained in words. Bring all of this into your energy field, from your feet to your head and your crown chakra. Let it instill in your energy field new possibilities for how the world can be, for how the Earth can thrive, how people can live together, in harmony with each other, with the planet. Be open to the role you will play in this great evolution, this beautiful transformation. Be still. Witness.

Then, release your need to have an identity separate from the cosmos, a personality, a special something. Touch the bundle to the fire to burn it away.

Be still. Be.

Use the smoking bundle to cleanse your entire field, toe to head, of any traces of self-importance, of any you-ness. Make yourself invisible even to yourself as you cleanse that need to matter, to make a difference, to be remembered. And when you have done this, pause and simply be still.

After you have experienced this emptiness, touch the bundle to the fire, knowing that you are now bringing in the unmistakable knowledge that you are woven into the great field of creation and deeply loved, an expression of loving, divine wisdom. Bring in the energy to every part of your field, from your head, focusing on the crown chakra, and then moving on to the rest of your field, all your chakras, and your lower body, right down to your feet. Feel your connection to Mother Earth, to Pachamama.

Welcome how Spirit has crafted a journey that will be uniquely yours. Invite it in and embrace it, saying, "In this journey, in this lifetime, may I be of service to those that I meet along the path, however humble my actions may seem, however small my moments of service may appear."

Be still and open to the potential that surrounds you and all the potential that is within you.

And when you are ready, ask your power animal to have a conversation with you about what you need to know before ending this fire ceremony. Write or draw any answers you receive, thank your power animal for its help, extinguish the fire and the bundle, and close the sacred space.

CHAPTER 8

EAGLE WISDOM
(THE EAST)

Our team departed not long after sunrise. Skipped the pancakes made from a boxed mix and served with fake-sugar syrup and went for a walk by the river instead. Back home, I generally skip breakfast: it's in those morning hours when blood-sugar levels are at their lowest that the body goes into detox and we begin burning fat for fuel instead of glucose. Feeling a sense of vitality and clearheadedness, I was ready for the hike ahead. Our trek today would take us on a steep descent into a valley along a trail used by caravans for thousands of years.

The lore of Buddhism includes many tales of masters practicing their discipline and attaining enlightenment in solitary caves. Archaeologists have found more than 10,000 of these caves in Nepal, man-made burrows high in the side of mountains that offered refuge from thieves and marauders while serving as places of contemplation. Many of these "sky caves" line the steep valley walls of the ancient Silk Road along the Kali Gandaki River. We could see them high above us a few hours from Ghar Gumba. The trail was flat, with no trees that might offer refuge from the midday sun in this barren, high-altitude desert.

Joan turned to follow a small trickle of a stream that branched out from the river. After an hour or so, we started descending, following the rocky banks of the stream that gave way to a narrow canyon—a cleft in the mountains where the stream must have been fed from springs because it gathered volume. Around us, we began to see tall trees that had sunk their roots into the watercourse and provided a bit of shade.

Marcela and I, along with a few others on the team, stripped down to one layer of clothing by a shallow pool and took tentative, barefoot steps into the frigid water. I groaned in relief and pain at the soaking of my overheated feet, which were so swollen they seemed an entire shoe size larger than they were a few hours before. We waded in, carefully picking our way across the rocks into the deepest part of the pool where we could dunk our heads, the stinging cold a shock to our systems. I could barely get my body entirely below the surface as every cell in it was screaming in protest at the chill, but this was the first real bath we'd had in days.

In the Andes, I had learned a practice of observing my body in extreme cold, maintaining the awareness of my core heat even as my brain tried to push me into a state of panic. The trick was to relax into my breath, slowing my exhalation, making it last longer than my in-breath. The first few times I had tried it, I was unable to relax: I had hyperventilated and shaken uncontrollably outside my tent, shivering through layers of clothing. I keep trying, and after a while, with practice, I was able to reach a state of deep relaxation even with a thin shirt on despite the initial shock that always threatened to send me into a panic. Mine was not quite the tummo practice of the Tibetans, who could dry wet towels on their naked backs in the middle of winter in the Himalayas, but then, I was not interested in drying towels. I just wanted to learn to tame my fight-or-flight-or-freeze survival response.

I fell back on this training in the cold stream along the Silk Road, slowing my breath and heart rate even as I observed the tips of my fingers turning blue from the cold. The state of quiet mind from yesterday's ceremony returned to me. I was able to witness my mind not going into hyperdrive even as my physiology was responding to the tremendous stress of the icy water. This is the awareness I am determined to have someday in the future as I near the moment of my death. "Thank you, Medicine Buddha, for giving me this strength to remain present and witness," I murmured to myself.

Once dry and back in our clothes, we gathered again at the base of the hill that led to Guru Rinpoche's cave and began to select what to leave behind—daypacks, water bottles, anything that weighed us down.

"What else should I leave behind?" someone mused aloud.

"Any preconceptions as to what you are going to find," Joan quipped.

A good reminder of how we become enamored of every discovery as being of the utmost importance, every act yielding undeniable validation of how very worthwhile our efforts have been. Like children constantly seeking approval, we are always in need of reward, always attached to having a big "aha" moment, which makes it incredibly difficult to surrender to a simple experience. Why not raise the bar for myself and give up all expectations of something special happening farther up the trail, of having some important revelation?

We entered the cavern. It was huge, like the inside of a circus tent, with a stone promontory in the center that seemed to have seats carved into it. Two heavyset monks at the entrance beckoned us inside, bearing candles whose light joined that of multiple tapers set about the cave, which cast an eerie glow on the ceiling. The sweet, pungent odor of incense filled the air, almost covering any scent of the damp and dust that tickled my nostrils. As the flickering shadows danced before my eyes, a sense of the magical arose in me. Now you see it, now you don't—what would disappear and what would take its place? What might happen if I gave up the need to make it happen or have it happen? Maybe nothing. I was open to that possibility.

My eyes were still adjusting to the light when I felt a hand reaching toward me. I looked up: it was my friend Stephan inviting me to climb up a little farther and take a seat next to him. Stephan is a lifelong meditator, and it seemed like a good idea to be next to him so some of his good vibes would rub off on me.

Shortly before the trip, we had attended an ayahuasca ceremony together, one led by a Brazilian healer. Stephan and I were sitting next to each other, waiting for the effects of the visionary brew to kick in. I turned to him and asked, "Do you feel anything?"

He shook his head. "How about you?"

"Nope. Nothing."

And then the medicine hit both of us with a wallop.

With him next to me in Guru Rinpoche's cave, it seemed natural to turn to Stephan and ask, "Do you feel anything?"

It might have been the tone of my voice or some memory that set him off, but I could see he was trying not to laugh. Suddenly, I was doing the same, trying not to disturb any other practitioners around us.

And then it happened. The walls of the cave, which were dusty and damp, suddenly became warm and comforting. I felt myself in the womb of the Great Mother, held and comforted by the Earth herself. Here was all I needed. Here was the comfort of not-knowing yet knowing peace and possibility. . .

Timelessness.

The vastness of the cosmos and the smallness of Alberto.

When I opened my eyes a few minutes later and looked at the ceiling of the cave, I imagined I could see the night sky filled with stars, each one a Buddha realm, a world created by consciousness, that had turned the chaos of the cosmic dust of the universe into our familiar cosmos, into beauty and order. From seeming nothingness and disarray is born that which has gestated in the belly of the always-creating womb of the universe.

Eagle medicine is the gift of knowing that you are significant despite how very small you are. It's knowing that each step you take, each word you speak, can be an expression of love and that this lays the foundation for a new vision, a new way of being.

The shaman who has acquired eagle medicine lives her life with the perspective of the peaks and valleys and the curvature of the Earth, soaring over the land and taking in the big picture, the context for the details of life. She concerns herself with the crises her children are suffering, the pests destroying the village harvest, and the challenges facing all her people, yet she knows her task is to look to the horizon and beyond it to where opportunity lies. She is like the ancients who gazed into the distance to where the Earth met the sky and observed the subtle signs that encouraged them to journey in a particular direction, to a destiny beyond where the eye could see, a destiny the soul could recognize.

The promise of eagle medicine is vision, to free yourself of a continual focus on problems so that you open to possibilities. This is very difficult to do, for you have been trained from birth to find what's wrong, to pick up on flaws in others, on problems with your circumstances, or to notice a missed note in a symphony. When you focus on what's wrong, the universe will mirror back to you what you believe and what you perceive, and you will indeed live surrounded by messes and obstacles.

Deep down, many of us believe that if we can fix our problems, perfection will prevail, making us safe and happy. Suffering is part of the human condition; it is valuable and can help us to learn and evolve. Denial and the false security of toxic positivity aren't what any of us need. Beyond the erroneous hope that the clock can be turned back and the old normal reclaimed lies something extraordinary for us all.

Having mastered time and tasted invisibility as a result of doing the work of the North and hummingbird, the shaman enters into perfect ayni with the three worlds: the lower world, where she can access the wisdom of the past; the upper world, where she can engage with the sages of the future who offer guidance on crafting a fulfilling destiny; and the middle world, where she is a steward of the Earth and a keeper of wisdom. The gift of eagle vision is to be able to see the landscape for miles around yet spot the tiny mouse scurrying toward its hiding place far below and dive down toward it with precision, taking the perfect action at the perfect time. All the meditating and intention-setting in the world can't take the place of being in ayni with both the visible and invisible realms. You can't get caught up in everyday problems or sit on a meditation cushion forever. Before taking form in your mother's womb, you chose to be here, in this world, participating in life on Earth and acting as a steward and caretaker of the planet and a co-creator of our shared reality. At this time, more than ever, we are called to create a new vision, a new reality of life on Earth. Will you answer the call?

We don't need everyone to access the gift of eagle vision if we want to ensure that humanity's destiny on Earth involves evolution rather than extinction. We only need to reach a tipping point of *enough*: enough people transforming, evolving, and dreaming anew, freed from the suffocating grip of fate.

From Fate to a Chosen Destiny

Fate is what happens when our life trajectory falls within the momentum tunnel created by our genetics and our family drama. You and I began on a particular road as children, our destinies determined largely by our parents and communities. You can get off that bumpy road and choose a better one. Your health is strongly affected by lifestyle choices. You can affect your epigenetics (genetic expression) by what you eat, how much stress you live with, how you laugh, whether you forgive others—in other words, your mind and emotions play a powerful role. Shamans believe that upgrading the information in your energy field, which in turn changes your perceptions, feelings, thought processes, and mind-sets and affects your body and mood, is crucial. In this way, you can lighten the baggage and get off the road that leads to you dying young from heart disease or cancer or developing Alzheimer's. Those fates are fatal. They do not have to be yours.

The task is to free yourself from karmic influences and break family patterns. Do people in your family tend to end up alone in their old age? Do they usually prioritize their job over their families? When you see with the eyes of the eagle, you recognize that love can involve loss and hurt but that these do not have to define your future relationships. Eagle shows you how to let go of baggage created by being hurt by those you love. It shows you how to love yourself so you can love others and then find the beloved. You discover the love that offers you its wings to soar in joy and freedom.

Eagle helps you release the baggage of a job or career that is killing you slowly and find your true vocation, whether or not it pays all the bills. This will have a ripple effect on the people around you and your potential for gaining the courage to step into a preferable destiny for you.

If you're like most people, your spiritual baggage, which needs to be shed through the work of the eagle, is the mental confinement of religion or no religion. Eagle wisdom frees you to experience your spirituality without feeling pressured to deny what you have experienced in your free-form relationship with Spirit. It allows you to let go of the need to conform to others' ideas about the divine and your relationship with the quantum field. You cast off the heavy cloak of dogma that has locked you into a fate and out of a destiny.

You might have an awakening and realize that all you have been taught about having to go through a middleman to feel a sense of communion with God doesn't match with your experience. Yes, that mystical experience that you had when delivering your baby or walking in the woods during a psychedelic experience is a true revelation and epiphany. This might result in a sharp turn in your journey. Better to take a look at the religious load you're carrying and lighten it so you can make much-needed changes.

Fly Like the Eagle, Re-Sacralizing the World

Many believe that the sacred and the mundane are separate —or act as if they are. They mean to love themselves and others, but once they leave the weekend retreat or get off the forest path and climb back into their car, it's back to the old habits of trying to force the world to conform to their expectations. The eagle calls to us to bring the vision of beauty into our everyday lives, re-sacralizing them. As the Navajo Nightway song, a sacred chant, says:

> May their roads home be on the trail of peace,
>
> Happily may they all return,
>
> In beauty I walk.
>
> With beauty before me, I walk.
>
> With beauty behind me, I walk.
>
> With beauty above and about me, I walk.
>
> It is finished in beauty.
>
> It is finished in beauty.

To experience eagle medicine is to re-sacralize the world, to see the beauty in it even when what's in front of our eyes is hideous. In nature, there is violence, drought, and fire, which are necessary for creation and evolution, but these are not the only forces. When we're not in ayni, we only notice what has been taken away—the wonderful beach that was reclaimed by the rising waters of the lake or the lovable furry creatures ripped apart and devoured by the owl. We forget that nature replaces what gets taken away, replenishing the shoreline and the animal population. It's our primordial fear that makes us focus on losses instead of the larger natural processes of creativity, change, and evolution in the world and in our lives. It's our primordial fear that makes us forget our birthright and responsibility as co-creators of reality.

Don Manuel once asked me if I wanted to fly like an eagle or flap like a rooster as it stands on the roof of its coop. Did I want to soar the vast landscape or the barnyard full of chicken poop and feathers? Of course, I said I wanted the former. "Then you must let go of the comfort of the chicken coop—of regular feedings and shelter from the winds and the rains," he told me. "You have to let go of the protection of a farmer with a shotgun who will chase off any foxes that come to devour you."

That doesn't sound like an attractive or easy sacrifice. I liked my university job at the time, even though my dean regularly threatened to fire me and seemed intent on making my life utterly miserable. He did not believe in me or my work then. And I liked my comfortable family life despite my marriage being extremely difficult. But letting go is necessary if you want to fly.

We become attached to all that makes our lives easy, that offers us a sense of predictability and familiarity. If we're upset, we pathologize the experience we're having and hurry to find something to address the symptoms of our distress.

"To fly like an eagle," Don Manuel told me, "you have to let go of your insatiable thirst for comfort."

You can't receive the gift of eagle medicine without facing a few challenges.

Resisting Seductions, Releasing Attachments

In Buddhism, the way to enlightenment requires you to release your attachments. We have to recognize that we will eventually part with whatever we value in this life anyway. Even if we can hang on to our reputation, favorite activities, or mental faculties until our very last breath, when we die, we leave it all behind. Our attachments are seductive. Even the mere hint of safety and comfort can keep us stuck in the old ways.

Of course, we all appreciate the pleasures of this life, but they can distract us from our reason for being here: to awaken our medicine—our gifts—and be in service to the greater whole. It's our attachment to all that gives us pleasure, including our beliefs about our importance, that we have to be willing to let go of.

The notion of a destiny can produce a sense of grandiosity as we daydream about how we'll solve the world's problems. Some people will make their mark and be remembered for inventing something, starting a powerful movement, curing a disease, or something else of note. However, if you were to take a quiz on all the historical heroes you read about back in school, you would probably find that you've forgotten quite a few. And a hundred or a thousand years from now, will anyone remember the names of today's innovators? The truth is that for most people, their destiny won't be one for the history books.

The temptation is to want a far more impressive destiny than the one you're likely to have. Resist the seduction. That way, you'll stop missing opportunities to do the most influential work and stop wasting the energy you need to do it.

Seduction happens at every level of our experience. At the level of serpent, the physical, you can become seduced by good food, a nice home with central air-conditioning and amazing views of nature, great sex, or a fantastic salary and benefits package. It's possible to have all of these and not become attached to them, however. I used to think I couldn't live without coffee, and the smell of a good dark roast brewing accompanied by the scent of fresh baked goods right from the oven is hard to resist, but I also know I can live without these—and have. But when you are living with uncertainty, unsure of whether your favorite café will ever open again and your gut will ever repair itself enough to allow you to have a Danish with a good cup of java, it's harder to release your attachment even to this minor comfort. Honoring the uncertainty is difficult. But if you can do it, then you make room for the pleasure that comes from recognizing that there's much that you can live without as long as you do not lose track of your true nature. You are a spiritual being having a biological experience here on Earth as a human for a short time, and you are destined to return to the invisible realm where you originated. While you're here, you are likely to become distracted by all the pleasures available to you. Even so, it's possible to enjoy them while continuing to focus on the work you came to do: to live according to a destiny that honors the ancestors who came before and the ones who will come after you are long gone, and to be part of the unfolding of a sacred plan that includes all life on Earth.

At the level of jaguar, of emotions and thoughts, you can become seduced by feelings of acceptance and belonging. You might want nothing more than to be with people who shower you with affection and tell you how clever, wonderful, and lovable you are. But have you been seduced into staying in relationships that cause you and the other person to suffer? It's only when you're willing to let go of your need to be in a relationship where you get more than you give that it becomes easier to open up in your relationship with that person—or with someone else. Often, it seems easier to switch romantic partners or to create a new family of friends to replace your existing one. But if you're not willing to let go of the seductive notion of the perfect soul mate or family, you will end up bringing old stories into a new relationship. You'll look at the people who surround you and think, *How did I end up in the same painful dynamic with a partner I thought was completely different from my first spouse? How did I end up creating a circle of friends that squabble over the same arguments that my parents and siblings did?* It happened because you were seduced into thinking that you didn't have to change; you just had to change the people around you.

At the level of hummingbird, the sacred maps are many, but if you become too attached to one of them, too idealistic about living out a story that makes you feel important, you miss out on the potential for doing powerful, sacred work on behalf of all. You think you and your friends are going to change the world, but then everyone's anxiety about getting the slogans and sound bites right and who should be the spokesperson causes so much dissension that the cause gets lost and the movement dies. It's easy to become seduced by an idea or a movement while ignoring the fact that everyone has personal desires that can cause conflicts and trigger passions that lead to flash fires and scorched earth as people walk away hurt and resentful.

And you have to let go of our beliefs about hierarchy and perfect rulers, whether those rulers are an all-knowing, omnipotent deity or science and rationalism. Overindulging in spiritual practice to avoid the challenges of everyday life, leaving others to attend to them, is one of the seductions that the work of eagle helps you avoid. The other is embracing limited ideas about the nature of reality and your place within it that you inherited from religion and science. You might be drawn to particular maps, but if you become so enamored of an ideology that you have no flexibility when it comes to other maps, you'll find yourself stuck in the same old stories you wanted to shed and battles you vowed to stop fighting when you began the work of the medicine wheel.

The End to the Competition to Become "King of the Hill"

For too long, many of us have been playing the tired game of competition instead of recognizing the value of collaboration. Growing up, I would hear boys say to each other, "My dad can beat up your dad." Some people seem to want to brag that "my country can beat up your country." Patriarchy is not holistic. It divides up land and communities and pits neighbors against one another. Competition can have its upside, but as we participate in our evolutionary process to become *homo luminous*, we need to work together as a species, and with other species, so we can thrive into the future. We're being called upon to question the validity of competition as the primary organizing principle that determines our actions and survival. And we're being challenged to see how a perception that life is one big contest—whether it's a contest of who is more important or who has suffered the most or something else—can close us off to our natural senses. These senses open us up to greater collaboration with each other and the quantum field.

We're entering an era in which the feminine principle of nurturing and holistic living is making a comeback. We're beginning to remember that information, or knowledge, is different from wisdom. We can honor each other's feelings, beliefs, and perceptions while also recognizing that we all have biases that can skew our thinking and understanding. These are present even if they are invisible to us.

Wisdom is understanding that even the kindest person in the room will have biases. Ordinary perception and thinking has limitations—we have a need for help from a greater, wiser source. This is a source we cannot perceive with our ordinary senses or broach with our ordinary thinking. Wisdom requires that we come to our natural instincts that allow us to perceive our interconnectedness and interdependence within the field, to experience absolute truth instead of relative truth, which is what we mistake for "the truth" when our biases are influencing us.

Many of us decided at some point that we would look for the truth through the lens of science, which we expect to be free of bias and fear, a clear lens through which to understand our world and our experiences. If you rejected religion only to get caught up believing that science explains all, you're still stuck in dogmatic thinking. Science is not without flaws or biases. For one thing, scientific researchers face fierce competition in building their careers and reputations through producing genuine breakthroughs. That can cloud their perceptions. Richard Horton, the chief editor of the distinguished UK medical journal *The Lancet*, stated that "much of the scientific literature, perhaps half, may simply be untrue" and that "scientists too often sculpt their data to fit their preferred theory of the world." Acknowledging that studies might be flawed and that research from well-respected teams might be badly distorted by biases doesn't endear a researcher to their peers.[1]

How scientists set up their experiments can be heavily biased too. We still overlook the fact that most medical research has been conducted on white people of European descent and may not be applicable to people of all ethnic backgrounds. Too many pharmaceutical drugs have been tested only on men and the results applied to all people regardless of gender. Consequently, drugs such as Ambien (prescribed in the U.S. more than 40 million times last year) that are metabolized differently by women and men were prescribed to women in the wrong dosage—double the dose needed to bring about the intended effect. Researchers have often seen women with their fluctuating biology as men with complications, so to speak—as having hormones that would "screw up" the research if they participated in it. This attitude has begun to change to a more inclusive one only recently.

Research and evidence are important. That said, scientists are equally likely to cherry-pick what supports their old ideas and narratives that make them feel important compared to others. We don't recognize that scientific knowledge isn't the same as wisdom, that there are many ways of understanding the world and more types of medicine than the ones treated in a laboratory.

As we let go of our "king of the hill" mind-set of competition in science, as we release our need to be smarter and superior to others, we will see more collaboration and integration of different wisdom ways, perspectives, and means for bringing about healing and well-being for all. We will study phenomena that were previously overlooked. Years ago, scientists thought the duplicate coding on DNA was some sort of mistake. It turns out this "junk" DNA is involved in epigenetics. Like the 19th-century physicians who insisted that they didn't need to wash their hands or put out their cigar before performing surgery, scientists still have much to discover—and often, blinders to discard.

Eagle Medicine

We can become seduced by the illusion of safety that big ideas—democracy, unconditional love, miraculous cures, science, reason—offer us. All of that is good and valuable.

But all that seems light also has a shadow. The trick is to remain at enough of a distance from all these grand ideas to be available to the wisdom that can offer us a new map and compass for our lives and the future. The Tao says that the sign of a truly free man is that he is not seduced by his own preconceptions. Eagle vision liberates us from limited, distorted perception, letting us experience a much higher level of understanding than we imagined possible.

What you seek might be taking form right now while you are caught up in trying to make it happen. Remember, mastering time means letting go of old ideas of cause and effect and the past determining the future. Expecting perfection now instead of progress at a pace you're not in control of, progress as determined by something much larger than you, is a sign you've become mesmerized by your self-importance. Be willing to let go of your convictions and your attachment to seeing the fruits of your labor. Let go of the need to have your efforts validated and to see unmistakable evidence that you personally have made a difference.

And then the difference you make will occur.

At the level of eagle, we can become blinded by the light, seduced by the exquisite feeling of bliss that comes with experiencing oneness with Spirit. We long to remain absorbed into a deep pool of perfect joy, but soaking within it indefinitely isn't possible as long as we're here on Earth—unless we're willing to give up our sanity and leave it to others to take care of feeding us. We have to get up off the meditation cushion and take action when appropriate, channeling the sacred, creative, healing power of Spirit. Spirituality that isn't grounded in everyday life is like a mirage in the desert, promising sustenance but keeping you from your destiny and the joy of contributing in your own way to the Earth, her creatures, your community, and finally, yourself.

Meditation has its place, but it can also be an avoidance behavior. Once, I was explaining to Don Manuel that it's difficult for me to do sitting meditation, and he shook his head. "My people don't meditate in the 'shitting' position," he quipped. Meditation, I learned, is being mindfully present with all that we are offered, which could be a moment of action, speaking, performing a fire ceremony, or listening to someone else who may be saying more with their silence than with their words. This idea of taking time away from your life to meditate is tempting. How much more comfortable is it to sit on that cushion than it is to be present as someone you care about who is hurt and angry accuses you of all sorts of hideous behaviors? Bring the sacred into that moment of discomfort and pay attention to what arises from your acceptance. You can make yourself overthink or make yourself peaceful, stepping onto a sacred territory that will reveal where you might go if only you stopped running away from discomfort. Then you will know what to do and what not to do. You will not flail about. You will step into grace, seeing both the details of your life and the larger vision that you have co-created with Spirit.

The shamanic traditions do not attribute grace to saying a prayer or making a burned offering to a loving deity outside of you, separate from you. Instead, the power is available to anyone who enters into right relationship with nature. You establish and maintain a quality dialogue with the cosmos and speak to the rivers, trees, and God because it's your birthright. Then you enter into perfect ayni as you practice right action (yankay); right loving relationship to nature, yourself, and your neighbors (munay); and right thinking (yachay)—similar to the Buddhist Eightfold Path, which includes right speech, right action, and right thought.

Emptying Space That Eagle Medicine Can Fill

Set an intention to release your seductions and attachments at all levels—so you might experience absolute truth.

At the physical level, be willing to let go of comforts you have grown accustomed to—the foods you love, the sex you enjoy, the pleasure you take in dancing, listening to music, hiking, or smelling the rich scent of pine trees in the forest. Become open to sacrificing the comfort of electronics and all modern technology. Intend to release the physical stamina that gives you confidence that you have many healthy and productive years ahead of you.

You do not have to let go of these wonderful things forever. You simply have to be willing to do so for now to experience the emptiness that can free you to soar like an eagle.

At the mental and emotional level, be willing to give up the thoughts that bring you comfort, thoughts that you're a good person, an honest and hardworking individual, that you're smart and able to handle whatever life throws at you, that you are lovable and deserving love. All those affirmations you have repeated over the years about who you are, what you deserve, and what you are determined to manifest—surrender those so that you can open space for eagle medicine. Be ready to give up your feelings of contentment and irritation, your self-righteous anger and your pride in your accomplishments and all your successes.

You do not have to let go of these wonderful things forever. You simply must be willing to do it so you can soar.

At the mythic level, be willing to give up the big ideas that give you comfort in difficult times, that make you feel as if the world offers predictability. You'll be letting go of reassuring beliefs such as that God is looking out for you, that justice can prevail on Earth, and that good people who work hard will lead healthy, happy, prosperous lives.

You do not have to let go of these wonderful things for-ever. You simply must be willing to do it so you can soar.

At the level of Spirit, you will be ready to give up your beliefs about what spirituality is and is not and your under-standing of the nature of the cosmos that came to you because of your early learning. You will shed dogma so that you can simply experience your interconnectedness with the cosmos. You will give up your need to understand so that you can know awe and awaken your natural instincts, using them to guide you in your everyday life. You need to be able to let go of your dogmatic beliefs, including any beliefs about scientists having bias and spiritual leaders being com-pletely free of it. Then, if you're Christian or Jewish or iden-tify as a practitioner of some other religion, you'll find the light in the teachings instead of being confined by them.

You do not have to let go of these wonderful things for-ever. You simply must be willing to do it so you can soar.

Mystery is everywhere. Immerse yourself in it—but be careful not to make that a distraction from all that you need to explore and be in this world. Someone has to pay the bills, including the bills due to Mother Earth, who is exact-ing a price for the damage we've done to her. Just because you don't live in a coastal village under threat from violent hurricanes or on lands that experience wildfires doesn't mean that these are not your problems. We will all have to make changes to bring balance back to nature and help the Earth to heal. The repercussions of the work in the eagle will be felt at all the other levels: the mythic, the psychological, and the physical.

Be willing to release your comforts, your attachments to what you like and what makes you feel at home in your own skin, safe in your family and community, and opti-mistic about the future. Set the intention to feel the loss as you release your attachments at each level—physical, psychological, mythic, and energetic or spiritual—and to remain present in the feeling of being detached. You must grieve this loss for a shift within the architecture of your energy field to occur.

Once you have set the intention to surrender to the emptiness, free of attachments, no longer tempted by your seductions, you are ready to do the eagle fire ceremony. If you wonder, *Why should I do this?* or *What's in it for me?* be sure to surrender that thought before proceeding.

Fire Ceremony for Eagle

Prepare for the ceremony according to the instructions given for the hummingbird fire ceremony, and make sure you have a candle or fire, an herb bundle (lavender, sage, rosemary, or other dried herbs tied together), and a notebook and pen.

When you are ready, identify what you want to burn away—religious teachings you were told not to question and that never felt right to you, a devotion to science and logic that has made you rigid and dogmatic, a penchant for spending so much time in a state of bliss and so much effort at focusing on the spiritual that you have neglected everyday obligations to yourself, to others, to the Earth, and so on. Then, touch the bundle to the fire to release the energies connected to these inflexible, extreme ways that have given you a false sense of security. Bring the bundle to your energy field near your lower three chakras and cleanse them. Then cleanse your heart chakra. Release from your field the decrepit old ways.

Now touch the bundle to the flame a second time and bring the energy of the fire, of its transformative powers, into your lower chakras so that you can receive the seed and give birth to a new destiny, one free of the fates that have had you in their grip. Bring in the energy to every part of your field, from your head, focusing on the crown chakra, and then moving on to the rest of your field, and your lower body, right down to your feet. Feel your connection to Mother Earth, to Pachamama. Know that you are liberated from the seductions that have prevented you from opening to the mysteries of life. Know that now you are purified, free to experience your spiritual nature and natural instincts as you are meant to.

Welcome how Spirit has crafted for you a journey that is uniquely yours, invite it in and embrace it, saying, "In this journey, in this lifetime, may I be of service to those that I meet along the path, however humble my actions may seem, however small my moments of service may appear."

Be still and open to the potential that surrounds you and all the potential that is within you.

And when you are ready, have a conversation with your power animal. Is there any wisdom it has to share with you? Ask it whatever questions you have, and write down the answers. When you're ready, thank it for its help, extinguish the fire and the bundle, and close the sacred space.

As difficult as it is to do the work of the wisdom wheel, this is what will lead to your evolution—and to our evolution. Choose the healing, wisdom way, the way of the shaman, of the Earthkeeper, and climb the mountain one step at a time, using the fire ceremonies as your tool for transformation when working with the wisdom wheel. Evolve into the sage and visionary you were meant to be so you can own your power. Every step counts. Every breath can be a prayer as you reconnect with Mother Earth. Every act, every non-act, will cause the master within you to stir from its slumber. There is no time like the present to do the work of timelessness and to soar like an eagle among eagles.

AFTERWORD

Not long after the Nepal expedition you read about in this book, a client of mine, who operates eco-resorts around the world and a luxury hotel chain committed to sustainable and culturally sensitive tourism, called my office for a shamanic consultation. One of their lodges in the Indian Ocean was experiencing problems—water lines breaking, sewers overflowing, guests disgruntled, occupancy rates down—and nothing they had tried had helped turn this "bad luck" around. At their wits' end, they had decided to call a shaman. Shamans are excellent at helping those who are experiencing "bad luck," for we see it as simply "bad ayni": bad relationship with nature or with the ancestors.

I scheduled a remote session with the manager of the hotel, who explained that his 10-year-old son had been having terrible nightmares since they arrived on the island a few months back. The boy was dreaming of serpents coming out of the sea and threatening their home. Children are much more sensitive to the invisible world than adults, and the boy's nightmares gave me a clue to what was happening. When I tracked the dynamics of the minuscule island using my shamanic senses, I felt that the ecosystems had been disturbed by the construction of the hotel: the protector nagas in the sea had been angered.

I scheduled an intervention with Amchi's assistance because he is a master of the power of the nagas. He agreed to perform a Naga Puja, a ceremony for feeding and appeasing the creatures. Amchi, dressed in his full robes as a Buddhist priest, worked online from Nepal; I had invited my shaman friends in the Andes, and I joined in from the U.S. During the ceremony, Amchi offered yak milk and prayers while the Andean shamans prepared a medicine bundle with the flowers and seeds of the season to honor Pachamama, Mother Earth. At the end of the ceremony, Amchi instructed the boy to take a bowl of milk to the beach and leave it, along with an incense stick, for the nagas—and to say a prayer before he left his offering.

That night, the boy began to sleep peacefully once again. Within a week, the water leaks and sewage problems were fixed, occupancy began to increase, and a pending lawsuit with local authorities was resolved.

If I could fix all of our problems with a bowl of milk . . . I thought. But I knew that this was just the outer form of a powerful ceremony that reached into the invisible world where the forces of nature converge to create or destroy.

It's not the bowl of milk or the offerings in the ceremony that appease the nagas, for they are ancient beings dedicated to the protection of all creatures on the Earth. Instead, they want to help us become Earthkeepers, stewards of all life on Earth, and protect her forests and habitats. The ceremonies were not only for them but for us—to help us see how to co-create a better relationship with nature. You can't simply go to an island with bulldozers and construction crews, damage the ecosystem, and then call yourself an eco-friendly hotel because you recycle plastic water bottles.

Fortunately, this hotel group is committed to real eco-tourism and rose to the occasion, making the deep changes that would ensure a lasting positive relationship with the forests, the seas, and the local human and animal inhabitants.

An Evolutionary Leap

We are witnessing an era of history drawing to a close. Before us is the possibility of humanity developing a grand new understanding as it emerges into the "fifth sun," as the sages of Middle America describe this time. The Andean shamans believe that it is the time of prophesied reintegration of the peoples of the Four Directions. With their counterparts in other areas of the planet, Andean shamans are making offerings to Pachamama, Mother Earth. They do this to facilitate the bringing of a new order and harmony to the world. They hold that it is time to reawaken that sacred fire of their traditions and share it with the world to reunite all people.

The awakening I'm describing will be a global phenomenon, expanding exponentially as the few become many, as the people of all races become Earth stewards. But there's also a personal element to it. We can each choose to work through our personal issues that might whisper to us that, "I'm not good enough to do anything as important as all that," or "This sounds like feel-good spirituality, but what the shamans are talking about isn't real. . ." Believing you're not good enough and pure enough to do the work is a form of self-indulgence; the same is true of assuming the work isn't important enough for you to take it on. The maxim here is to bite off more than you believe you can chew, to find the entire desert in a grain of sand, and to say yes to the calling that has been softly whispering to you for some time.

As this regeneration of humanity gets underway, humankind can experience an evolutionary leap forward, a remaking of ourselves and the planet, but this will only happen if each of us discovers the magical, invisible realms through a shift in our perceptions and the architecture of our energy field. We can most easily make this energetic shift when we're in nature, but we can also do it indoors by drawing on intentionality, personal power, and love to engage with

Mother Nature. This is called the return to the mother—that mother that never left us and that wants us to be well.

To do this, we must shed our toxic beliefs about having to look out for number one only, whether "number one" is ourselves, our family, our community, or our country. We have to release any attachment to a specific outcome that might be beneficial to us but harmful to others. We have to serve something greater than our own desires. Only then will we see our desires being met.

As you are finishing this book, ask yourself what you need to do to become an Earthkeeper—and not do. If you know, get your mind out of the way and take action to align with the sacred plan encoded in the tides and eddies of the quantum field. Begin your work to serve this plan, for the gifts await, the medicine you have been seeking that will help us all to heal and to dream into being our new bodies and our new world.

APPENDIX

The Invocation:
Working within Sacred Space

Whenever I practice shamanic work, I create a sacred space that is free of the distractions of the middle world, of my everyday busyness, a place where I can experience a quieting of the mind's activity as I surrender to what is happening moment to moment. Sacred space serves as a platform for interacting with the quantum field, with Spirit in its four emanations—serpent, jaguar, hummingbird, and eagle— and in the forms of Father Sky above us and Mother Earth below us. As the shaman within the circle, you represent the point where the energies converge to help you in your work.

Honor these powers by summoning them respectfully. Affirm their presence as you turn to face each direction. I rattle or drum as I do the calling to create sacred space—and again when closing it, thanking the forces for their help. You can shake the rattle or strike the drum once, sharply, before moving on to address the next direction as you continue to create sacred space or close it after your work is completed. I suggest working within sacred space when you do the fire ceremonies or the power animal exercise in this book.

Doing this will allow in only the highest of the subtle energies from the invisible world.

While many of us are familiar with prayer from our religious upbringing, it's important to understand that this "prayer" is actually an invocation that summons the four fundamental forces or powers of nature. They take on the power animal forms that we associate with them, but they are much more than that. They are the four forces that make up all of creation. After you complete your work, release them once again that they may return to their formless state in nature. When you forget to close sacred space and release these forces, they will create disorder instead of bringing order and beauty.

The following invocation is the one that I use when creating sacred space. You are welcome to use it until you find your own words.

The Great Invocation

To the winds of the South

Great Serpent, Mother of the Waters,

We call on you, Mother,

Come and wrap your coils of light around us

Teach us your ways

To shed the past the way you shed your skin

Teach us the beauty way, to walk with beauty on the Earth

To grow new bodies, to heal, so that we might evolve into *homo luminous*

To touch everyone we touch with beauty

Ho!

To the winds of the West

Mother, Sister Jaguar,

Come to us, walk among us

Teach us your ways of fearlessness

Of gentleness

Teach us the ways beyond death

Beyond fear so that we might step into the unknown with trust, so that we might become valiant explorers

Be with us

Ho!

To the winds of the North

Hummingbird, Ancient Ones,

Guardians and keepers of this land

We call on you

We come to honor you today

Hummingbird, teach us to find stillness in flight, to practice ayni with nature and the ancestors, so that we might become sages and draw on their wisdom

We call on you, Grandmothers and Grandfathers

In your name, we gather

Be with us

Ho!

To the winds of the East

The place of the rising sun

Mother Eagle, Sister Eagle, Condor,

Come to us from your mountaintop and soar with us

Hold us sweetly under your wing,

Teach us your ways of flight, of vision so that we may
become visionaries,

Dreaming a new dream

Ho!

Pachamama, Great Mother, Mother Earth

We come to you, Mother

Thank you for your breath, for your waters

And to all our relations

The stone people, the plant people, the creepy-crawlies

The winged, the furred, the finned

All our relations

Ho!

Father Sun, Grandmother Moon

To all the star nations, our star brothers and sisters

The sacred mountains of this land, of this Earth

Great Spirit,

You are known by a thousand names

You who are the unnameable one

You who sit above us and below us

You who sit in the North and the South

And the East and the West

Thank you for allowing me to sing the
song of life one more day

Ho!

CLOSING

To the winds of the South

Great Serpent, Mother of the Waters,

Thank you for teaching us your ways

The way of shedding the past the way you shed your skin

Thank you for being with us

Ho!

To the winds of the West

Mother, Sister Jaguar,

Thank you, Mother,

For teaching us the ways of fearlessness

For teaching us to journey to infinity

Accompany us as we go back to our homes, and our villages

And our loved ones

Ho!

To the winds of the North

Hummingbird, thank you for teaching us to drink deeply
from the nectar of life

Grandmothers, Grandfathers,

We honor you

And we gather to honor you who will come after us

Our children's children

Thank you for being with us

Ho!

To the winds of the East
The place of the rising sun
Eagle, Condor, thank you, Mother,
For holding us sweetly under your wings
For nudging us out of the nest when our time comes
That we might find our own wings
And always fly wing to wing with the Great Spirit
Ho!

Pachamama, Great Mother, Mother Earth,
Thank you for all of your blessings
For your breath and your waters
And to all our relations
The stone people, the plant people, the creepy-crawlies
The winged, the furred, the finned
All our relations
Ho!

Father Sun, Grandmother Moon,
To all the star nations
Our star brothers and sisters
The sacred mountains of this Earth
To Great Spirit, Creator of All,
You who are known by a thousand names
And you whose name cannot be said or told
Thank you for blessing us in all ways.

ENDNOTES

Chapter 3

1. Joan Halifax, *The Fruitful Darkness: A Journey Through Buddhist Practice and Tribal Wisdom* (New York: Grove Press, 1993), 53.

2. Alberto Villoldo and Erik Jendresen, *Island of the Sun: Mastering the Inca Medicine Wheel* (New York: HarperCollins, 1992), 175.

Chapter 4

1. Brian G. Dias and Kerry J. Ressler. "Parental Olfactory Experience Influences Behavior and Neural Structure in Subsequent Generations," *Nature Neuroscience*, 17 (2014): 89–96, doi: 10.1038/nn.3594.

2. Rachel Yehuda et al. "Holocaust Exposure Induced Intergenerational Effects on FKBP5 Methylation," *Biological Psychiatry*, 80, no.5 (2016): 372-80, doi: 10.1016/j.biopsych.2015.08.005.

Chapter 5

1. Martha Henriques, "Can the Legacy of Trauma Be Passed Down the Generations?" BBC, accessed March 26, 2019, https://www.bbc.com/future/article/20190326-what-is-epigenetics, and Andrew Curry, "A Painful Legacy: Parents' Emotional Trauma May Change Their Children's Biology. Studies in Mice Show How," Science.org, accessed July 18, 2019, https://www.science.org/content/article/parents-emotional-trauma-may-change-their-children-s-biology-studies-mice-show-how.

Chapter 7

1. Christopher and Barbara Johnson, "Menominee Forest Keepers,"
    American Forests Magazine, April 27, 2012. https://www
    .americanforests.org/magazine/article/menominee-forest-keepers/.

Chapter 8

1. Richard Horton, "Offline: What Is Medicine's 5 Sigma?" *The Lancet*,
    385, no. 9976 (April 2015): 1380. https://www.thelancet.com
    /journals/lancet/article/PIIS0140-6736(15)60696-1/.

ACKNOWLEDGMENTS

An immense and immeasurably deep bow of gratitude to my editors Nancy Peske, Patty Gift, and Anna Cooperberg. They worked the earthen clay, giving it shape and form, and share the credit for the vessel that became this book. And I am indebted to the wisdom keepers of the Andes who so generously shared their stories and wisdom with me over the last five decades.

ABOUT THE AUTHOR

Alberto Villoldo, Ph.D., has trained as a psychologist and medical anthropologist, and has studied the healing practices of the Amazon and Andean shamans. Dr. Villoldo directs the Four Winds Society, where he trains individuals in the practice of shamanic energy medicine. He is the founder of the Light Body School, which has campuses in New York, California, Chile, and Germany. He directs the Center for Energy Medicine, where he investigates and practices the neuroscience of enlightenment. Dr. Villoldo has written numerous best-selling books, including *Shaman, Healer, Sage*; *The Four Insights*; *Courageous Dreaming*; *Power Up Your Brain*; and *One Spirit Medicine*.

Website: thefourwinds.com

CONNECT WITH
HAY HOUSE
ONLINE

🌐 hayhouse.co.uk   **f** @hayhouse

📷 @hayhouseuk   🐦 @hayhouseuk

▶ @hayhouseuk   ♪ @hayhouseuk

'The gateways to wisdom and knowledge are always open.'

Louise Hay